Horsin' Around A Lot

STU CAMPBELL

Second Printing 2004
ISBN 0-9675164-0-4

Distributed by Johnson Books
1880 South 57th Court
Boulder, Colorado 80301
E-Mail: books@jpcolorado.com
www.johnsonbooks.com

PRINTED IN THE UNITED STATES OF AMERICA

Johnson Printing Company
1880 South 57th Court
Boulder, Colorado 80301

Contents

Rough String Rider

When I got out of the Army, I went back to Nevada figuring on getting on with a good cow outfit and making a living in the saddle again. I didn't have any trouble getting on an outfit as it was early March and the ranches were looking for buckaroos to go out on the wagon.

I got a pretty good string of horses and was getting used to long hours in the saddle again. My roping was getting better–three years in the Army doesn't help anyone's roping. And seeing as I wasn't much good before I went in the Army, I figured I was getting better as I was catching a few every now and then. But my roping practice was mostly practice coiling my rope. Some of the boys was watching me heel calves one morning and one of them remarked that the reason I wasn't catching many was 'cause I was jerking up my slack too fast. I told him that if them calves wanted to be caught by me they'd have to get faster themselves.

That's the way it was. We all laughed and had a good time. We was having such a good time, in fact, that I was beginning to wonder if I was pulling my share of the load. I was bringing in a lot of cattle and the boys was more than patient with my roping, but I kinda felt that I should be doing something more.

So, moving into the corral one morning, I says to the cow boss, who was roping out everyone's mount for the day, "Bill, if you'll lend me a snaffle bit, I'll start riding some of them colts." Well, he says "yes," and ropes out a big bay colt for me. As I'm leading this horse out of the corral, Bill says he'll help me get him saddled when he's done. I thought this was kinda strange, but I knew what he meant about 20 minutes later when the colt had broken my hobbles and was standing on top of a hill with my saddle under his belly. I sure felt foolish. The only thing I felt good about was that I wasn't in the saddle, being in the position it was in.

Well, we got the horse back and the saddle wasn't worse for wear. It had been through some rough spots before and I didn't notice any new scars on it, so pretty soon, I was mounted and doing a day's work.

This horse–think his name was Clyde or Claude, or something like that–well, him and me, we got along pretty good together once I was on or off him. The problem was getting on or off, cause that's when he'd buck, and that's when a cowboy is most liable to get hurt cause his balance might not be so good.

On this day, we got along good until it came time to get off. We'd been leading a gentle old pack horse with us, planning on dropping him off at a line shack and picking up another, but time had run short on us. So I was elected to take the pack horse up to the shack. Seeing as how I had three or four wire gates to go through, and Clyde (or Claude) was hard to get on and off, I decided to switch horses, as it might mean the difference between walking and riding later on.

Needless to say, Clyde (or Claude) jerked away from me and I was stranded with nothing but a pack horse and a halter. The only thing I could do was ride the pack horse bareback and catch up to my saddle.

There isn't much use for a horse trained to ride bareback on a Nevada cattle ranch and I wasn't half on until I found myself all the way off. Well, there I was. I'd started out with two horses and now I was afoot.

But I managed to catch both horses when Clyde (or Claude) caught the end of the soft cotton rope I was using for reins between two rocks. And I finally managed to get the horses traded.

I found out later from some of the boys that Clyde (or Claude) was supposed to be the roughest horse on the ranch to ride at that time. But for me that day, that gentle old pack horse wasn't no slouch.

For Medicinal Use
ONLY !

The old-timers talk about how a bottle of "high spirits" was a cure-all for most kinds of ailments in cattle, horses and men. The medicinal value of whiskey and other hard liquor isn't mentioned much any more, but they do have some value.

I had a neighbor one time who kept a calf alive for a week on straight whiskey. The calf had a bad case of the scours and was dehydrated pretty bad, but he pulled him through. So, when I had a colt come down with a pretty bad case of diarrhea, and the commercial preparations I tried didn't have much success, I decided to try whiskey.

I don't usually keep any whiskey on hand so I had to go all the way into town to get a bottle. I was beginning to wonder if this colt was worth all the time and money I was spending on him. I found a liquor store and figured it would be pretty easy to get some whiskey and get home to finish my chores.

There was some old guy looking over the selection in the corner and he turned with a surprised look on his face when I walked in. The clerk behind the counter looked kind of surprised too. Then I figured out why.

Before I came into town, I'd been working some cows and calves and I still had my chaps and spurs on. I began to feel somewhat self-conscious, but, I'd come for some medicine for that colt and I figured I'd better get it.

The surprised look had disappeared from the clerk's face and as I walked up to the counter, he said, "What can I do for you sir?".

I told him I wanted a bottle of whiskey. That old guy over in the corner was still looking at me and I was not only self-conscious, but I was beginning to get nervous.

The clerk asked me what kind of whiskey I wanted and I said, "I don't know mister. Anything my colt will drink." The old guy over in the corner looked a little more surprised and the clerk looked like he was both amused and bewildered. He was looking over his glasses when he says, "What does your colt prefer?" He was kinda laughing when he said it and the little old guy in the corner had moved closer.

Well, I was standing there scratching my head and I says, "I don't know—he's never had any before." That little old guy was laughing now and I had some thoughts about how I could make his little red face redder, but I thought better of it and decided to do some explaining. So, I says, "Well mister, you see, I got this sick colt at home an' nothin' else seemed to work so I thought I'd try some whiskey."

The clerk was still grinning as he says, "Medicinal purposes, huh?"

"Yes sir," I said, "He's a mighty sick colt."

He pulled down a bottle from the shelf behind him and showed it to me. "How about this? It's 96 proof. I use it myself, for colds," he said, still grinning.

"How would it be for scours? That's diarrhea in humans," I says.

"So, diarrhea is your problem" the clerk said.

"No!," I says, "Diarrhea isn't my problem, it's my colt's." Then I went on to explain how someone had told me whiskey used to be used and how my neighbor saved a calf with the scours using whiskey, and how colts need the liquid to keep from dehydrating. I was gonna tell him how I was worried about pneumonia and other complications, but I decided not to cloud up a somewhat foggy issue.

The little red-faced guy wasn't laughing now, but he was listening mighty close when the clerk says, "I guess if this is good for colds, it's good for about anything. How much do you need?"

I was going to ask him about the dosage for a four-day-old colt, but decided he didn't know anything more about it than I did. So I figured I'd get two bottles, 'cause I didn't want to go through this again, and I could give what I didn't use to somebody for a Christmas present. "Two," I said.

That little old guy started laughing and the clerk had a mighty big grin as I paid for the two bottles of whiskey.

As I was leaving I heard the clerk saying something about not being trained as a pharmacist and the old man laughing about how he was sick all the time. But I got what I went for and pulled that colt through.

Right now, I'm wondering how I will explain to the IRS man the purchase of one bottle whiskey for nursing a sick colt and one bottle for a Christmas present, in the middle of May!

Teton Shuffleboard

When a cowboy sees somebody walking toward him with two shovels, he's got a mighty good idea his roping and riding is over for the rest of the day. More than likely, he'll try to disappear for the rest of the afternoon.

I was wishing I could disappear one afternoon a few years back when I was foreman on the Bar B C, a dude ranch up in the Grand Teton National Park in Wyoming. There wasn't anybody walking toward me with a shovel, but I knew, as foreman, that: it was my duty to be walking to somebody with that cursed object in my hand. We'd been pretty busy taking out rides and caring for horses and guests and we had sorta neglected our cleanup work. The horse corrals were pretty dirty and, seeing as nobody wanted to go for a ride this particular afternoon, I thought it might be an opportunity to clean up them corrals some. Well, I didn't really think this was an opportunity, but the job had to be done and we had the time.

So, I got Scott and Ed, the two hired hands, and we started hunting up shovels. Scott and Ed found shovels pretty fast and I was thinking them two fellows might have to do this job by themselves, but Ed found another one. I guess with all my problems running that outfit, I hadn't really concentrated on what I was doing and walked right by one a couple of times.

We had three shovels and three men so we put the shovels in the pickup and started out. That pickup had traveled faster than it was going, but there didn't seem to be any rush. We took a swing around by the swimming hole and there was a lot of guests there and they invited us in for a swim. I was sorely tempted, but decided against it as, if I went swimming, Scott and Ed wouldn't clean up the corral. Besides that, I didn't know how. So I declined on the grounds that I never went swimming before in my life. Scott and Ed volunteered to teach me. But this was corral-cleaning day, so we left the swimming hole and was just pulling around the last cabin between us and the corrals when someone hollared, "Hey, what you guys doing?"

"Just killing time," hollars back Scott.

"Mighty poor way to kill time," Ed muttered as I got out of the truck. I figured we had time to confab some, so we walked up to the porch so as we wouldn't have to shout.

Walking up to the porch, I recognized Jerry, one of our guests (you always refer to dudes on a dude ranch as guests), sitting on his porch, his feet propped up on the railing, a book in one hand and a cold beer in the other. He looked mighty comfortable as compared to what I figured I'd look like when we got them corrals clean.

"Interest you fellows in a beer?" Jerry was already on his way to get it. Scott and Ed had already made themselves mighty "homey" in some big soft chairs and I was finding a soft spot on the pine pole railing when Jerry brought the beer.

"What are you guys really doing?" Jerry asked.

Ed started to say something about cleaning corrals, but I stopped him by saying, "We was just going to play some Teton Shuffleboard."

"Teton Shuffleboard?" Asked Jerry. "Is that anything like regular shuffleboard?"

I explained to him that Teton Shuffleboard was a game invented by the cowboys around the Tetons. As for how it compared to regular shuffleboard, I didn't know.

Then Jerry says how he'd been on a cruise one time and had been the champion of the whole ship playing shuffleboard. He told me that the idea of shuffleboard was to put your puck on a certain place and move your opponent's out of position.

Well, I allowed that Teton Shuffleboard was similar, but harder as the point of the game was to put more pucks on one spot without moving your opponent's pucks

Jerry thought this might be kind of an interesting game, and when I told him how Scott was the champion of the ranch and Ed and me had challenged him to a playoff for the championship, he showed more interest. I told him the pucks we used were different 'cause we had to make do with what was on hand, and the sticks might have funny shapes, but he seemed to figure we was all up against the same odds and he wanted to play. He was mighty interested in playing, but when I told him how this was a playoff for the championship and we only had three sticks, he seemed kind of disappointed.

Now, I always figured a dude ranch foreman's job was not only to take care of the horses and cattle, but to keep the dudes busy if they wanted to do something. It was getting mighty plain to me that Jerry wanted to do something, so I volunteered my shovel–that is, stick–and offered to keep time and score. Well, he was willing to play and as Ed, Scott and myself headed for the truck, Jerry went in the cabin for a few more beers and we headed out. Jerry didn't notice the shovels in the back of the pickup, but he started paying attention when Scott opened the gate to the corrals and I backed the pickup in. Then he started to get the idea, not completely, but he had some serious thoughts.

I explained as I handed out the shovels that I would keep score, as I didn't really have an interest in the championship. I also explained that the idea was to get as many of them "pucks" in the truck as possible, and that this was a timed event. Well, Jerry seen right then and there that he'd been took, but I guess he decided it wasn't so bad after all, and he really got in there and worked. When it came time to quit, Jerry had a bigger pile of manure in the back of the truck than either Scott or Ed. I tried to tell Jerry that he had to unload what he loaded, but he didn't seem too excited about the idea. Scott and Ed didn't seem too enthusiastic about unloading either, but I convinced them it was the thing to do, and Jerry sat under some aspens drinking a beer. I found myself on the working end of Jerry's shovel and was wishing he hadn't made such a big pile.

We decided that everyone on the ranch should have an opportunity at this game, so Jerry, knowing he had been taken in, kept quiet about the whole deal and in a few days we had four contestants who thought they could put up a fight for the championship, and even a bunch of kids who wanted to try.

So we decided to hold a contest to determine a grand champion of Teton Shuffleboard, a senior division and a junior division for the kids. Every kid would get a prize if he played. For the adults the prize was to be a trophy. Scott, Ed and myself had found an old whiskey bottle that had a nice shape, filled it full or corral dust and pasted on a label that read:

GRAND CHAMPION
of
Teton Shuffleboard
Bar B C Ranch   Moose, Wyoming

We held the kids' class first and it was a lot of fun. Most kids got more manure on themselves than they did in the truck. The kids did all right and the spectators enjoyed it and didn't have no favorites.

But when it came to the adults, there was a rootin' section for each man. We only had four contestants, and each had his wife, children, in-laws and friends rootin' for him.

For the big contest, we had moved to a bigger corral where more "pucks" were available. To receive the trophy, the winner had to make the biggest pile in the corral. I was trying my darndest to get them to pile the "pucks" in the truck, but each contestant argued that he was going to make such a big pile it would be hard to tell the winner. In the interest of fairness I consented and figured it would be easy to convince the losers not only to shovel their own piles in the truck, but in respect for the "champ," they could shovel his pile in too!

I finally determined, after a very spirited race, that Jerry was the winner. He had a bigger pile of horse manure in that corral than I thought it would hold. And there was three more that was right sizable too!

So we awarded the trophy to Jerry. Somebody hollared to Jerry, "Speech! Speech!" And Jerry said a few words about how he'd never have been able to do it without the help of the horses. Everybody left for a "victory celebration" at Jerry's.

I hadn't noticed, but the other contestants and Scott and Ed had left during Jerry's speech. I turned around to encourage them to start loading the truck, but they were gone and I was faced with loading the four piles into the pickup myself.

I started loading the truck, trying to figure out if Jerry had taken me or if I had taken him. When I'd made three trips to the dump, loaded the fourth and had it halfway unloaded, I knew I'd been taken by Jerry, 'cause him, Scott and Ed, the other three contestants and all the spectators showed up and sat under the aspens drinking their beers, watching me unload that truck.

Rarin' To Go

The Raft River Roping Club, up here in Malta, Idaho, holds a roping practice every Tuesday and Saturday night. I ain't a member, but the club lets nonmembers rope for two bits a run. They mostly team rope. I'd been down to watch a few times and everybody asked why I didn't bring a horse.

Well, I didn't have a horse. I ain't owned any horses since before I went in the Army. Fellers would volunteer to loan me their horses, but I always declined 'cause I felt funny about borrowing things.

I had a good horse out at work, and I asked the superintendent if I could run him down one of these nights. He said "fine." I'd roped some with him and he done OK. I was the one having troubles–catching the stock and getting my dallies.

Here it was Saturday night and I was asking Jerry, my partner at work, if he was planning on roping tonight, and if he was I'd buy him a run or two if he would haul my horse down. He was putting on his hat before I'd finished asking him. .

Next thing I knew, I had my horse saddled and loaded and we was on our way to a roping. We unloaded the horses, got some tickets and was figuring on roping some steers for practice.

Somebody must have seen me coming, 'cause when we rode into the arena, he hollered, "Anybody want to jackpot?" Jerry said something about needing a steer or two to practice on and somebody else said, "They don't need any practice, they been roping all day."

I had taken my rope down during the day. I had to rope a calf and doctor him for an eye infection and when the little feller run into my loop and I'd caught him, I was so surprised I'd forgot all about taking any dallies. I got my rope back and doctored that calf, but I figured I needed at least one steer to catch and see if I could still dally.

There was two steers left in the chute, so l told the guy running the gate we would take the second one, seeing as how some other team was already in the boxes.

Well, our steer come out and Jerry caught the head. I spurred my horse out of the chute so fast that I about run right over Jerry's rope and the steer. Almost had a wreck there, but we recovered and I threw two pretty bad loops at the heels. I guess they was bad loops 'cause I didn't come up with anything.

Jerry 'n me entered the jackpot. I think it only cost a dollar a team for two steers. We was pretty near the last team to come out and everything was in our favor. I'd seen them other teams rope better than that, but I guess everybody was having a bad night. The way things was going on this go-round, all a team had to do was catch 'em legal and they had a fair chance of winning.

On the first go-round, Jerry missed the head loop and I didn't even consider throwing my rope, 'cause we was only allowed two loops.

The second go-round was about the same as the first. Them fellers was having a rough time catching heads 'n heels.

Our turn come and Jerry made a mighty nice catch on that steer. I was coming in for the heels and I heard Jerry saying, "Take your time, take your time." Good thing he said that 'cause I could see I was coming in a little fast, so I slowed my horse down some, come and laid my trap.

There was a lot of dust in that arena and I couldn't see if I had caught both hind legs, one hind leg, or missed. But I could see Jerry moving that steer forward and I figured if I was going to catch anything that night, I'd better take up my slack. I figured we was in the money.

I was just taking up my slack. I could see I had at least one hind leg and was turning my horse to face the steer and started to take my dallies when all of a sudden my horse started rearing. He just wasn't lifting his front feet off the ground, he was trying out for some movie part! I had some worries about him coming over backwards.

I could hear the other contestants and spectators yelling, "Ride him! Stick with him!". I could also hear Jerry yelling, "Dally, dally!".

Right now I was in a predicament. I didn't know whether to dally or leave that saddle horn alone so as I'd have something to hold onto if I needed it. Besides that, my horse wasn't facing the steer. That horse would rear and every time he come down, I'd start to turn him back to the right to face and he'd rear again.

Turning to the right wasn't one of his best moves, although he'd got some better at it during the last few months. He hadn't pulled a stunt like this for a long time.

Leastways, I got him settled down, took my dallies and faced him to the steer. We was lined up, ropes tight and I seen the flag go down. Then I looked down to survey the situation.

I still had one hind leg, but my rope come up between the horse's front legs. I guess when he reared, his right front leg come down over the rope. Maybe that's what caused him to continue to rear.

As for him rearing the first time, I don't know what caused that. I think maybe the horse was kind of excited, but then I may have jerked on him rather than turning him, in my own excitement. Maybe I got to seeing too many dollars. I don't know, but the feller taking off the ropes in the catch chute was saying, "Leastways he rode him." I guess it was quite a sight.

Needless to say, we wasn't in the money. After it was over, I went and checked on the winning times, just to see what they was, and I come away thinking, "Even with the five-second penalty we might have been in the money if me and my horse hadn't of put on a show by ourselves." With all the action we provided, we still turned in a time of 42.5, penalty and all. Not a very good time, but an exciting time.

Jerry and me was loading our horses, laughing and talking about what happened, and I says to him, "Jerry, maybe we ought to plan on coming up next week, Tuesday night."

"Oh?," says Jerry.

"Yep," I answers. "It took me a couple of throws to catch one, but I did, and even with the horse trouble I had, we still turned in a time. Besides that, my horse can use the practice, and me too."

"You gonna use the same horse?"

"Yep. Leastways we're catching 'em, and I'm hot."

"Your horse and you is 'just rarin' to go'," says Jerry.

"You bet! Just rarin." That's exactly what we'd done and how I felt about chasin' out another one.

Where The Action Is

When I was young I remember my dad saying something like "The kind of country your mother comes from, they have to go to a zoo to see cows!" Mother was from Philadelphia, Pennsylvania, to be exact, and it wasn't her fault she married a cowboy who took her to Utah.

I'd been back East to visit mother's relatives but was pretty young at the time and didn't remember much. Here it was some 20-odd years later and I was on the East Coast doing active duty in the Army. Mostly at mother's insistence, I took a few weeks and went up to get acquainted with aunts, uncles and cousins I never met. Leastways I didn't remember meeting them. This was in the last part of August and early September.

I don't guess every family in "Philly" has a cowboy for a nephew or cousin and maybe I got to telling them I was a better bronc rider than I was.

Well, it ended up that I was going to ride in the last rodeo of the season at Cowtown, New Jersey and all mother's folks was going to see me win some big money for a little work.

I'd tried a few bulls and broncs at the Cowtown rodeo earlier during the summer and I'd seen the rodeo on television a few years before when I'd got busted up some working on an outfit up in Idaho. I wasn't busted up bad but the doc had given the cook orders that I was to stay in bed long enough to let a few bones mend.

Now the cook on this outfit wasn't a person to be messed with. She was a big woman who took a lot of pride in what she cooked and how she took care of the cowboys. On that outfit there was always a cowboy or two laid up for some reason or another. The horses were pretty rough, but the old gal knew what was best for the hands when they was in her care, and she could be just as rough or rougher than the horses, so most of the hands didn't argue none–not even the boss. So I took a couple of weeks' rest.

I was getting better, though I don't know how. I wasn't getting no coffee–tea the old gal would bring me. I wasn't getting any meat either but I sure had a lot of soup and I even had some kind of mush for breakfast. I didn't like it but I knew how onery that old gal could get, so I ate it and didn't say nothing. She didn't say anything but she must have knowed I was getting restless cause she'd come in every Saturday to change the channels on the TV set and watch the rodeo from Cowtown with me. I'd get kinda excited watching that rodeo and say something about some-body bucking off 'cause he had too short a buck rein, or that horse bucks like ol' Sugar or that guy made a good ride but he missed the horse out of the chutes.

Well, the old gal was sharper than I was cause she'd say, "That horse didn't buck like Sugar, more like Drifter, and that feller didn't miss him out, he marked him, but he didn't miss him! He just didn't score good enough to place." I found it hard to believe and hated to admit it but the old gal knew more about bronc riding that I did. I finally ended up by saying, "If I ever get back to that place I'm going to ride in that rodeo–and I don't mean the grand entry!"

She says, "Yeh! And if you draw that horse you think bucks like Sugar, you'll buck off. But if you ride him like Drifter, you'll win."

Here it was years later. My mother's relatives, friends and associates was at Cowtown, waiting for me to come out and show the fellers how we do it out West.

I was behind the chutes, waiting for my name to be called. The horse I'd drawed was a chute-fighter, but it wasn't too hard to get the saddle on and he was acting about half-decent now. But the hard times was to come when I set down in the saddle. Right now I was relaxing, having a smoke and for some reason, thinking about the cook on that outfit up in Idaho. I didn't know if this rodeo was televised or not, but I was hoping if it was that she would be watching. I was thinking it might be nice if she was taking care of some poor, broke-up cowboy, filling him full of tea, soup and mush when she heard my name on TV, coming out on some money-winning bronc.

My name was called and I got mounted. Considering the reputation of the horse, I didn't have much trouble getting set in the saddle–the horse was saving his energy for later.

Anyways, I was set on my horse, asked for the gate, blew a stirrup and bucked off. The horse bucked right on past me when I'd bucked off and I was laying there in the arena, brushing dirt out of my hair and wiggling my toes (something I always done first after I bucked off). I could see my uncle Charley sitting in the grandstand with all my other aunts, uncles, cousins and their friends around him. As I got up I could hear the announcer saying something like, "And all that cowboy from Salt Lake City gets for his try is your round of applause." I heard hands clapping, uncomfortably close. I looked up and all the clapping was coming from the people around uncle Charley. The only people applauding was my relatives. I accepted their applause by tipping my hat and bowing and the clown chased me out of the arena. The clown chasing me brought a bigger applause than my effort. I guess I had to run pretty fast to get away from him.

I still had a chance to show everyone how good I was. The bull riding was coming up and I'd drawed a good bull and I figured I could ride him.

Eventually my turn come at the bull riding. I asked for the gate and the bull came out. He spun back around to his left for a couple of jumps, straightened out for a couple of jumps, then spun around to his right and tossed me off.

I didn't waste no time wiggling my toes on the ground–done that on the run. I hit the fence, made the top rail and then looked back to see what was happening. The clown had drawed the bull off and the announcer was saying, "And all Stu Campbell gets for his efforts is… "Well, I'd heard something like that before. Clapping was coming from right behind me. I turned around to thank them folks who was applauding and there was my uncle Charley. No, he hadn't moved. I quickly checked the spot where I fell off my bull and it wasn't six inches away from where I'd bucked off my saddle bronc.

I made a hasty retreat to the back of the chutes and recovered my gear. The rodeo was over and except for some rerides, most folks was leaving. I was figuring on doing the same until uncle Charley caught me.

Next thing I knew I was right in the middle of what seemed like a thousand people, most of them relatives. I signed all the kids' programs and one little girl says, "I hope you don't mind, but I'm glad you fell off. My daddy always told me to cheer for the underdog."

I told her I didn't mind and I realized that I probably exaggerated my abilities some and might have put it on a little thick.

Uncle Charley asked me what happened. After my realization that I may have enlarged my abilities some, I sure didn't want to say the horse and bull bucked me off fair and square, honest and clean. So I just said, "I fell off right in front of you so as you could see 'where the action is!' " He said "thanks" and we all went back to Philly.

Pedro The Rope Horse

I was working down in Utah one time and only about half satisfied I was doing both the farming and the cowboying and was about running myself to death.

I was using company horses, that is horse, on this outfit. He was the only one they had and I sure felt sorry for him. They called him Pedro and I had to use him for everything.

He was a pretty good built horse and real stout but he wasn't much on reining. I had to rope a one-eyed cow one day and we was going full speed. I got the cow roped, got my dallies and by the time I had Pedro stopped, we'd passed the cow and drug her about 20 yards. I figured this cow weighed about 1,100 pounds and I was right pleased to have her on the end of the rope, acting as an anchor, because I was beginning to wonder if I could get Pedro stopped.

I could see then that Pedro needed some more education, so every time I used him we did some drill work. His problem wasn't only that he didn't know how, but he'd never been taught the finer points of stopping and turning.

I started teaching him a little every time I rode him. He was learning but I could see that he would never be an outstanding cow horse. As long as we could get the job done right without too much stress on the cattle it was OK. I didn't much care how professional we looked as long as we could get the work done.

Time come for the fall gather and I was trying to give Pedro all the rest time I could because I figured I'd be bringing most of the cows home by myself .

The owners and managers of the place brought their friends and neighbors out to help gather the cows. We looked more like a circus rather than a bunch of riders looking for cows when we started out.

I studied the riders and their horses and come to the conclusion that there would be a lot of saddle sores on both horses and people. It didn't appear that they would really be that much help.

Before we even started to gather cattle we found a cow that had stuck her foot through her neck chain. I set out to rope her and take the chain off, but it took me four loops to catch her. I was really mad at myself. Here I had an audience to show off how good a roper I was and how well Pedro worked a rope. He had improved considerably but we couldn't put on much of a show. When the other people got to where Pedro and I had caught the cow, I was fashionin' a neck rope. I'd half-hitched the rope around the saddle horn and hobbled Pedro. Pedro would hold the cow.

Nobody wanted to heel the cow so I borrowed someone's horse and caught the heels after a few throws. I sure wasn't bragging about my roping abilities. But then, them folks wasn't saying what a good roper I was either.

We gathered quite a few cows that day, but I purposely left one cow and her calf up on the mountain. The cow had a bad case of foot rot and I knew she couldn't make it home. I would just have to go back up in the truck, rope her and drag her into the truck.

Pedro had had a pretty rough day but the drive up to the cow gave him a little rest. I found a bank of dirt where I could unload Pedro and maybe get that cow and calf loaded.

I roped the calf first, figuring the cow wouldn't be able to get far away. I caught the calf on the first loop. Seems like I do my best roping when nobody is around.

Getting the calf into the truck was a job, but we managed. I tied the calf up in there, and his racket almost scared off the cow. I roped the cow and drove her over by the truck. I thought we might have some trouble getting the cow in, but when she saw her calf in there she jumped right in.

Pedro did right well working the rope that day. But I remember a day I took my rope down and then because of the circumstances decided not to use it.

One of our bulls had gotten out one night and the next morning I saddled Pedro and went out to get him in. I figured it would be pretty easy but didn't count on the amorous intentions of the bull toward some heifers.

We started the bull back towards home three times, but each time he'd turn back and get by us. The third time he just about run over Pedro and me so I decided if he tried that again I'd drop a loop over his horns and show him I could get a little rank too!

So, I took my rope down and started the bull home again. The bull turned again. This time, as I was getting ready to rope him, he hit Pedro. Old Pedro stood there just like a brick wall.

The bull had hit Pedro in the shoulder and I could feel one horn on the inside of my boot, pinning my ankle against Pedro. I still had my rope ready but passed my chance to rope the bull. I sure didn't want to rope him while his horn was in my boot.

I ended up getting the bull home by taking all his girlfriends with him. Pedro wasn't any worse for wear but I had a big hole in my boot.

Getting On A Horse,
More Or Less

When I graduated from high school I left home and got a job on a cattle and dude ranch in Montana. I had never worked on a dude ranch before and didn't really know what to expect.

The first three weeks on the Ox-Yoke Ranch at Emigrant went pretty much like they would on any other ranch. We had some cows to move around, a lot of horses to shoe and we put in a lot of wood for the summer and following winter.

The boss drove away one day and when he returned he had a carload of people. The dudes, that is "guests," had arrived.

The next morning, Jim, the boss, briefed me while we were bringing in the horses. I'd never thought much about it but getting on a horse can be a problem for some people. I always get on according to the horse.

Jim was refreshing my memory about the use of the mounting block. We had the horses in, and as Jim was finishing what he was saying about how dudes get on horses, he casually said something about "good hands not even needing the cinch tight and not needing them done up to get on a horse."

I told Jim I'd sure like to see that. He declined, since "This might not be the best horse to show off on."

I remembered this incident about 10 years later, when I was foreman on the Bar B C Ranch, a dude ranch in the Grand Teton National Park in Wyoming.

One day I was really getting mad watching the "guests" get on their horses. They must have thought the purpose of the saddle horn was solely to help in getting on and off. They would grab the horn to drag themselves up, almost pulling the saddle off.

Watching the dudes get mounted, I thought of a woman I had watched getting on a horse at another dude outfit. This woman must have weighed 250 pounds. She and her family wanted to go for a ride, just for an hour or so. Looking at the horse the boss had picked for this gal, I figured it would take an hour or so just to get her mounted. The boss on this outfit always picked the biggest, stoutest horses for the biggest, fattest people, and rightly so. But it was mighty hard to get them mounted. In this case, the four of us finally got her up.

To get her mounted, one of the ranch hands held the horse by the reins. I was on the off side, putting all my weight on the right stirrup and another fellow was pushing against the swells and saddle horn on the left side. Pete was helping her get her foot into the stirrup.

She was started up. The horse was kind of giving-in to her weight. I was straining to keep that saddle in place and the fellow on the left side was doing his best, too. But we were fighting a losing battle–the saddle was slipping and we thought the gal was going to pull the whole works over.

Pete was right handly though. His quick thinking prevented a possible disaster. He seen what was happening and got right in there and put his *shoulder to the wheel*. At least, he put it where it would do the most good, and he just about lifted the woman onto the horse by himself.

This incident was what I was thinking about that morning, watching the dudes get mounted at the Bar B C. I figured it was time to impress on them the right way to get on a horse.

"What's going on here?" I said as I walked into the center of the group. Sometimes, if you do it right, you can be mighty gruff with dudes and get away with it–especially when you've got something to teach 'em.

"I have been watching you people get on your horses and there ain't none of you that knows beans about it," I said. "Get off them horses and I'll show you how to get on a horse the right way. Pay attention, 'cause I don't want to see none of you dudes pullin' them saddles off them horses!" They all laughed when I called them dudes. That was good.

I showed them how to get on, then I told them. I had them tell me, and try it themselves. Then I showed them again.

I was sitting on my horse, telling the dudes that it was just a matter of coordination, balance and timing. "Heck," I said as I was getting off, "Most good hands don't even tighten their cinches as tight as yours unless they are planning on doing some heavy roping. Good hands can get on a horse with the cinches hanging!" I was remembering what Jim had said many years before at the Ox-Yoke.

"I'd like to see that," someone said. It was the boss lady, Mrs. Corse. She had been watching.

I was in trouble. I'd dropped a casual remark and now I was being called on it. "This might not be the horse to do that on," I said. But I was thinking–this horse had good withers and he would stand, he wouldn't turn into you when you were mounting.

"Go ahead, Stu, show them how." It was Mrs. Corse again.

"OK," I said, "But first I'll get on with the cinches done up and you watch and see if it's any different than when I get on with the cinches hangin'."

I mounted, maybe a little slower than usual, thinking about just how I did it so I wouldn't make any mistakes later. I got off the horse and let the cinches hang. "Now you people see if I can get on this horse without the cinches done up and see if I do it any different than the way I just got on." I started to mount and much to my own amazement, as well as the dudes, I ended up on the horse, in the saddle, rather than on the ground with the saddle on me.

I didn't spend much time on the horse with the cinches loose. I quickly got off and told them dudes that if they was going riding that day, "They'd better get mounted the right way and get goin'!"

I was real relieved and tickled to death that the little stunt I pulled came off. I was thinking about doing some betting with the dudes that had not seen it but decided against it. I had been lucky one time and that was enough.

Just the other day, at work in the feedlot here in Southern Idaho, I let the superintendent borrow my horse to bring up a few cattle for branding. He put his foot in the stirrup and pulled the saddle off to the side. I usually don't tighten the cinches too much unless I am going to do some roping or hard riding. The horse didn't have good withers anyway, so if you were not paying attention, the saddle would roll.

As I was watching him reset the saddle and take the cinches up, I heard him muttering something about "That darn Stu and his loose cinches." I was thinking about showing him how to mount a horse the right way. But this sure wasn't the right horse to show off on.

Catching A Horse

Getting your hands on a horse for the day's work or just an afternoon ride can sometimes be a day's job in itself. Most horses can be caught fairly easy but some have their oddities.

Bill Kane, cowboss on Stanley Ellison's Spanish Ranch in Nevada, had a horse in his string that was kinda hard to catch, unless you knew how.

Bill was called away for a few minutes one morning, and seeing as Frank Moon and myself had our horses caught and saddled, he asked us if we would catch this horse for him–I think his name was Kilo. Frank and I both knew the horse and didn't think much about a job as simple as catching a horse.

There was probably 40 or 50 head of horses in that corral and each time we singled out this horse he would get away from us. He was wise to the ways of the rope and would duck away from the loop at the last second. Frank and me was still trying to catch that horse when Bill came back. He'd only been gone about 20 minutes and he smiled when he seen Frank and me still trying to catch that horse.

I gave Bill the rope and told him I'd about throwed my arm out trying to catch that horse. He was still grinning as he took the rope and just tossed it over Kilo's back. He didn't make a loop, but that old pony froze in his tracks.

Kilo just stood there while Bill haltered him and coiled his rope. "This horse is broke 'old timer style'," Bill said as he led the horse out. After that I started taking more notice of how Bill caught his horses. Every time he decided to ride Kilo he'd catch him the same way. And the horse never tried to get away as long as that rope was laying across his back.

I trained a horse to stand still, to be caught and bridled one time, but I had to get kinda rough with him, according to the way some people do it. I was working up in Wyoming for a company that specialized, among other things, in trail rides. My job, along with four or five other guys, was to guide people on one, two or three-hour rides and point out things of interest.

Consequently, we spent a lot of time in the office waiting for folks to come in for a ride. When people did come in for a ride we usually got the horses that were the easiest to catch.

One day all the other fellows were out on rides and I was the only one left in the office. A bunch of folks came in wanting to go riding. I sized up the customers and decided I had enough horses with big saddles that I could take everyone out for a few hours. But it meant that I would have to use a big black gelding named 'Mormon.'

Now Mormon wasn't a bad horse. As a matter of fact he was a good dude horse. But he was hard to catch and even harder to bridle. When a feller went to put the bit in his mouth, Mormon would raise his head as high as he could, making it almost impossible for anyone under 6-foot-2 to bridle him.

I'm only about 5-10 and figured I'd have a time, not only catching Mormon, but bridling him too. I decided to get everyone else's horse caught and get them mounted—and then I'd catch Mormon. The person I'd decided to mount on Mormon was a girl, and she probably outweighed my 150 pounds by 30 pounds or more.

Catching Mormon was a job, but I finally got it done by roping him, after all else had failed. I dallied him to a fence post.

Getting him bridled was a different matter. I started to bridle him and up went his head. I knew I was fighting a losing battle, and even if I won I'd still be the loser, since Mormon would be just as bad or worse to bridle the next time. I decided to do something about it.

While Mormon was holdin' his head up, making it impossible to bridle him, I decided a left jab to the jaw would show him I meant business. But I thought about it again and decided a left jab wouldn't do any good—a hard left blow to the jaw would be better. I tried the hard left blow. Naturally, Mormon backed off, but I held onto the lead to stop him.

I heard some comments from the dudes that was already mounted, but they didn't bother me, so I started to bridle Mormon again. Up went his head. I popped him in the jaw again. This time the gal that was supposed to ride him started into the corral saying something about "mistreating that horse!" One of the policies of the ranch was that dudes wasn't allowed in the corrals—for their own safety. And even though this gal outweighed me by 30 pounds, I told her that I had to discipline this horse some and she didn't have no business in that corral. I put her outside the corral and went to bridle Mormon again. He raised his head. I popped him in the jaw again, but this time I pulled the bit into his mouth and over his ears as I did it. Mormon was finally bridled and saddled.

On the ride I did some thinking. I had used the same treatment on another horse up in Montana that was also hard to bridle. Like Mormon, I had finally convinced the horse to accept the bit. That settled it—I decided to use Mormon every chance I got and use the same treatment when necessary. I was pretty sure I'd have to sock him every time I bridled him. I wasn't sure how long my hand would hold up, but I had made up my mind to do it.

During the next week I used Mormon every chance I got. I soon realized that he was easier to catch if I called his name when I wanted him. And after a few "treatments" of the sock in the jaw, I found that if I walked into the corral, called his name and held my hand up in a fist, he was very easy to catch. He even held his head down, making it easy to bridle him.

I didn't have any more trouble with Mormon after that, but the other fellows still had a hard time catching him. Even though I showed them how, it seemed to me like they wasn't sincere when they held up a fist and called "Mormon."

My Wife—
the unlikely bronc rider

My wife, originally a city girl, used to think cowboys were a thing of the past, out of work since the last Indian uprising. She thought people in big hats and boots were truck drivers, parade riders or movie stars. She thought horses were used for parades and hay rides. Then I come on the scene.

I was in town, takin' a few days off and gettin' some supplies. I figured I cut a real dashing figure wearing the new clothes I'd bought, and I set out to have a night on the town. I didn't have a date but I had run into an old friend who knew some gals, and I talked him into callin' them.

It was a blind date. I'd never seen the gals before and by the time they got to where we were supposed to meet them, my eyesight was gettin' kinda blurred. I thought maybe I was having too good a time, but after the girls showed up, I spent more time dancin' than drinkin' and worked it out of my system.

I guess I'd done too much dancin' out in the country 'cause I was sure bumping into people and stepping on people's toes. After the first three or four dances people started giving us a little room, and we sure had a good time.

My trips into town became a little more regular and it wasn't long before Mary and I had set a date. I quit the ranch where I was workin' and decided to start college again. With the money I'd saved, and taking a few broncs to ride on the side, I got through one summer and one winter.

The following spring we run out of money when I paid tuition. I started looking around for a good ranch job but couldn't find one where there was facilities for a man and wife. I finally managed to get a job giving trail rides at a resort area in a national park in Wyoming. Mary got a job cleaning up cabins.

I worked seven days a week at giving dudes rides, showing them the country and wildlife and answering questions about horses. Mary worked six days a week, and on her day off she would come over to the corrals to watch the horses. This was really the first time she had been around horses, and she didn't get very close at first.

Occasionally, if there was an extra horse, I would give Mary a free ride for an hour or two. The other wranglers would also give their wives or girl friends free rides, and Mary learned a little about horses, riding and talking with these gals. Mary got to looking forward to her days off so she could go for a ride. She became real disappointed if there wasn't an extra horse around when she showed up.

On this outfit we had a moonlight ride, where for $5, a person could rent a horse to ride out and cook a hot dog and ride back to the corrals watching the moon come up.

Mary really liked this "hot dog" ride and she'd usually go when I had to take one out. I used a lot of care in selecting a horse for Mary to ride. I wanted a better-than-average dude horse. I finally chose a yellow gelding they called Pal.

Pal wasn't really too bad a horse, as dude horses go. He was built pretty good, gentle and he even neck-reined some. I figured he'd be a good horse for Mary.

With Mary on Pal and everyone else mounted, we started out. I was elected to lead the group. The other wrangler, Walt, would ride alongside the single file riders, reminding them to keep a hold on their reins and not let their feet slip all the way through the stirrups.

This was usually an uneventful ride. The horses would be a little tired after working most of the day, and the only excitement would be seeing some unexpected wildlife.

We went down a wash and up the other side. Knowing that most of the horses would trot down this little wash, I stopped and hollered back to the dudes to take a short rein and a good hold on the saddle horn. Walt rode up where he could see every rider and be handy if someone started having some troubles.

I had the smaller kids behind me and we made it all right, so I didn't even look around to see how the older folks made it. I just kept going.

As we were nearing the picnic grounds where we would cook the hot dogs, Walt came ridin' up. "You didn't tell me Mary was a bronc rider."

"She ain't," I answered. "What happened?"

Horsin' Around A Lot

"Old Pal really bucked going down that wash. Didn't you hear him? He was bawling and really tearing up the ground, but Mary rode him."

I hadn't heard Pal. I was telling some kid how I used to be an outlaw and rode with the Jesse James gang, holding up stages, robbing banks and stealin' horses. The kid was really believing this tall tale and I was sorta enjoyin' it myself. I hadn't heard the horse bucking.

When we got to the picnic area and had everyone off their horses eatin' a hot dog, I asked Mary about her bronc riding. "No," she said, "The horse wasn't bucking, he was just loping."

"No," said Walt, who was listening, "He wasn't bucking, he was just tearing up the earth with everything he had. He'd put a lot of horses to shame in their buckin' ability."

"You mean he was really bucking?" Asked Mary.

"You bet he was!" Answered Walt. "And don't you let him try it again on the way back."

"I thought he was just loping," said Mary. "If I had known he was bucking I would have fell off. Good thing I didn't know. No, I won't let him try that on the way back." Mary's voice had a touch of amazement in it.

But she let the horse buck again coming down the wash on the way home. And she rode him again.

I let her unsaddle Pal when we got back. When she was done she turned to me and said, "That is sure a good horse. You ought to ride a few more bucking horses. That sure is fun."

Hard Day's Luck

Some days a feller shouldn't even get out of bed. I had one of those days not long ago. It started out pretty good—saddled my best horse that morning—but that was the only thing I did right.

We have a replacement heifer breeding program at the feedlot where I work in Southern Idaho. One of my jobs is to check the heifers early in the morning and late in evening and pull those that are in heat so we can breed them artificially. We usually have from 1,500 to 2,500 head to breed during a period of 45 days in May and June.

On this morning I was getting heifers out of the pens and keeping my eye open for one in particular. She was kind of wild. We'd had her out in the cattle alley the night before but she'd got past Gordon, the yard superintendent, and myself, a couple of times. We left her in the pen when it got dark.

I spotted her again the next morning and managed to work her out the gate with 15 or 20 other heifers. But she was a little wilder than I thought because she just about knocked over my horse Partner, trying to get back into the pen. Partner recovered but not fast enough to stop the heifer from getting into the pen. She'd done this a few times the night before and it was getting to be a habit with her. I was taking my rope down as I headed her back to the cattle alley. Partner stayed right with her as I built my loop and put her out in the alley.

It never occurred to me that I could close the gate and cut this wild heifer down the cattle alley where I wanted her. I had my rope down and meant to teach her a lesson. When I was done with her, she would be as gentle as a milk cow's calf or the wildest heifer in the state of Idaho.

She started back. Partner put his head down to head her, but this heifer wouldn't be turned. She put her own head down and tried to run over both of us. She hit Partner in the neck and knocked him off balance, but his reflexes were fast and he didn't go all the way down. He was back on his feet so fast he almost threw me out of the saddle.

We was right on the tail of that heifer and I was just about ready to throw my rope but I started to pull up. We was headed right for the middle of the pen and there were cattle still bedded down there. I figured we might have a wreck but Partner headed the heifer before we got too far into the bedded down cattle. He had to jump one heifer that was just startin' to get up and he didn't quite clear her. While we didn't have the big wreck I thought we would, he must have run 20 yards on his knees to keep from falling over and still keep up with the heifer we was chasing. He must have wanted that heifer more than I did.

As we closed in on the heifer, I glanced over my shoulder at the one we'd jumped. I figured we'd rolled her over and maybe hurt her, but she was standing up looking around with a dazed expression.

We headed the heifer we were chasing into an open spot. I was thinkin' I ought to stop and tighten my cinch some but I had a chance to get that heifer and I took it. I didn't dally up though, 'cause she was headed for the north side of the water trough and Partner and me was headed for the south side. So, when I should have been dallying, I flipped the rope over the water trough and the heifer put a foot through the loop.

I dallied up anyways, thinking, if she broke a leg or two, or even her neck, I'd take a lot of pleasure barbecuing her during the summer. She was headed west, around a big pile of manure the farm hands had piled up last winter. I headed Partner south, after laying a trip, planning on bustin' that heifer real good in the middle of that pile.

I was trying to figure out what I'd do to her when I got her down. My slack was coming up and I was counting on busting that heifer about four feet in the air when she hit the end of the rope. I was looking back when the heifer hit the end of the rope, but she didn't get busted. Instead, I felt the saddle turning. Without wasting any time, I chucked the rope and quit the saddle. It was hanging over on Partner's right side and it was either bail out or risk getting dragged. I didn't have much of a chance to select a place to land, though, and I ended up in the manure pile, where I wanted that heifer.

I caught up Partner and reset the saddle, taking the cinch up an extra hole. The heifer still had my rope around her neck, with a front leg through the loop. All I could do now was drive the heifer into the cattle alley, get the end of my rope, dally up and then really teach that heifer a lesson.

I got my rope, dallied to the saddle horn, and was just climbing into the saddle as the heifer come back past us. I got set, took an extra wrap around the horn and braced. Partner would hold her, even as fast as she was going. I figured we could set her back on her tail just like a little calf. But she hit the end of the rope and just kept goin', pickin' up more speed. I had to duck to miss the busted end of my rope as it come sailing back toward me. The way it was coiling I thought the heifer was trying to hang me with my own rope.

The short end of my rope was still on the heifer, but was working off. When it finally fell off, I got it, figuring I had either a mighty short lariat or a mighty long lead rope. But I had the heifer where I wanted her.

I caught Partner and loosened the cinch. That was when I noticed that my cinch ring had separated. It was egg-shaped now and there was about an inch of daylight where the ends should have met.

When I changed horses I got an old, but usable, cinch and another rope from the saddle shed. I caught up a colt I'd been foolin' with and started out.

I didn't get far before I had to open a gate, and while I was doing it my rope got hooked on the latch. The colt jerked away, the rope strap broke, the rope fell on the ground and the colt spooked.

I pulled on the reins to stop the horse but nothing was happening. I kept pulling—it wasn't a hard pull, there was no resistance—and takin' a shorter hold on the one rein to get the horse circling to stop him.

I'd been kinda crawlin' hand-over-hand up them reins, but pretty soon I couldn't go no farther—I was holdin' the snaffle bit in my hand! I was so surprised I could have swallowed it. Somehow or another I had busted the headstall on that gate and hadn't noticed it. I'd been watching where the horse was goin' so as when he come to a fence and had to turn I would turn the same way with him. I sure didn't want to lose him, or so I thought.

The colt was still spooked some and running, but not quite so fast. I still had some control on his head—the browband and throat latch was still on and the buckle on the cheekstrap kept it from sliding completely through and off.

I was turning the colt some, but we was coming to the fence. I kinda slacked up but that was a mistake—the horse gained a little speed. We was goin' too fast to turn and the way it looked to me we had three alternatives, all bad. The first was that the horse might try to go over the fence. This wasn't too pleasing to me because it was a pretty tall fence and if he did make it, I still wouldn't have him stopped. The second alternative was that he might try to go through the fence. This was even less pleasin' to me, because while it might have stopped him it probably would have crippled both of us. The third alternative was certain death, and I remember thinkin' as he tried to stop and turn at the same time, and all four feet went out from under him, "The damn fool's tryin' to do it! He's tryin' to go UNDER the fence!"

As the horse went down I cleared my stirrups and tried to get as free as possible, but I was a little slow and caught one ankle under the horse.

As I was sittin' there in the dust, I come to the conclusion that I'd probably broke my ankle. It was bound to happen. After all, I'd busted up everything but myself that day.

I got up and tried the foot. It seemed to work but it was mighty tender. I gathered up my rope and what was left of my rope strap and hobbled over to the saddle shed to get my hackamore. As I was approachin', the superintendent came by and said, "Stu, looks like you've had a rough day. Why don't you take tomorrow off?"

"Well sir," I said, "The way my luck has been running today I might need a day just to get my equipment back into shape. And if my luck don't change, tomorrow I'll be ridin' bareback usin' a halter for a bridle and bailing twine for reins."

32   **Horsin' Around A Lot**

The Squealer
and what I finally learned from him

A cowboy rides a lot of horses on the different outfits he rides for, some good horses and some not so good horses. But I think the best horse I ever rode wasn't even on a cow outfit. He belonged to a friend of mine, Dewitt Palmer, who lives in Millville, Utah.

Dewitt is a plumber, but I come to find out that he's one heck of a horse trainer. The room full of trophies he showed me bore this out. While he doesn't make his living in the stock industry, he has his horses and 10 or 15 calves that he used to bring his horses into shape. They also brought in a little extra cash in the fall and beef for the winter.

I had rented Dewitt's pasture for the winter to feed some calves in. I was attending Utah State University in Logan, and kind of thought the extra money them calves would bring in the spring would be mighty useful.

It was a pretty good winter for feedin' calves, not too much bad weather and one day along in February, Dewitt came up to me and says, "How would you like to do some cow cuttin' tonight? The ground's thawed out. We could turn on the lights in the arena and get in some early practice. We could use some of your calves if you want to. We won't get too 'western' and it won't be too hard on them."

"Sure," I said, "But I don't have a horse."

"You can use ol' Tink," he says.

"But I don't want to use your horse and maybe spoil him or sour him. I've never rode one of these expensive horses and I'd sure hate to ruin him for you," I says. All Dewitt's horses are registered. Ol' Tink's registered name is Tiny Dee and he goes back to Tinky Poo, a stud known in the Intermountain area for his "cow."

"You can't hurt old Tink," Dewitt answered.

So that night I found myself settin' my saddle on Dewitt's old cuttin' horse Tink. As we was gettin' mounted, Dewitt says, "You better warm him up Stu, you don't want him to buck you off do you?"

I sure didn't want nothin' to do with gettin' bucked off so I started lopin' him around the arena. I had watched them do this at rodeos and I figured I was doin' OK until I heard somebody say, "Make that horse get in the right lead!" It was Dewitt's wife, Louise. Right then's when I started gettin' a whole new education.

On the outfits I'd worked, I'd never paid much attention to what lead the horse was in or even if the horse was doin' everything exactly right. We'd get the job done and never pay much attention to how it was done.

Well, I come to find out how to make Tink get in the correct lead and how to make a proper rollback—by stopping the horse, pivoting him and then starting out as fast as he would go. All this was mighty educational to me and as I was learning, I kept thinkin' about some of the good old cow ponies I'd rode and how they kinda had to improvise over rocks, sagebrush and around trees. I got to wonderin' if them horses could work cattle in the open and if Dewitt's horses could work cattle in the sagebrush and rocks. So I asked Dewitt.

"Yep," he says, "But there's a difference. When you're workin' cattle out on the range, maybe sortin' out strays, you've got to get what cattle you want away from the herd and over to the "cut." There's some cuttin' involved, but most of this is drivin' cattle, takin' them where you want them."

"Right," I says.

"In cow cuttin' contests, we're takin' an animal out of the herd and holdin' it—not takin' it anywheres, just holdin' it. There's not much driving the animal. We're showin' how well and how fast our horses can turn and hold and out-think a cow. On the range, to get a critter where you want it, you've got to do some driving. Let's do some cuttin' now and you'll see what I mean."

So we got eight or ten head in and started to do some cuttin'. Dewitt went in first on Burley Joe Dee, a stud he owns that's gettin' to be real popular around Northern Utah.

Watchin' Dewitt and Joe work was just like gettin' into a horse show and being part of it for free. I was enjoying my watchin' so much that I forgot my job—turnback man. Dewitt was callin' for me to turn back that animal so as his horse could work proper.

Shocked back into being a participant rather than a spectator, I moved ol' Tink up to move that steer for Dewitt, but I wasn't figuring on ol' Tink.

When that steer moved, Tink moved right with him—only faster. I wasn't prepared and it's a good thing I've got a big horn on my saddle. I purt-near choked that horn to death tryin' to stay on. I finally got righted in the saddle and hoped Dewitt hadn't seen.

But he had. When he come up to give his horse a breather, he says, "Ol' Tink almost lost you, didn't he."

"Yep," I says, kinda quiet.

"Well, don't worry about it. There's been quite a few fellers fall off him and he's went right on and worked the cow."

I looked down at the old horse with new respect. "By golly," I thought, "You're not goin' to lose me so as you can have all the fun by yourself."

"Go in there and cut one out," Dewitt was sayin'.

By the time I'd selected a steer and worked him out of the herd, I'd got the best hold I could on the horn and was ready for anything, I thought. I'd never been on a horse that could stop, turn, dodge, spin and run so fast in my life. And it seemed like he done all this at once. I never been so close to bein' off a horse and still on it in my life.

I thought I was doin' right good just to stay on the horse, but I heard

Dewitt hollerin', "Let go of the reins! He can do it by himself!" I was so busy tryin' to stay on, I didn't realize that I was also tryin' to rein the horse.

Dewitt was right. Tink could do it on his own. "Maybe," I thought, "I could do a better job of stayin' on if I held on with both hands." I gave the horse more slack and took a better hold, with both hands.

We worked the steer some more 'til Dewitt thought we'd done enough and called us in. I was pleased to pull Tink up. He was breathin' kinda hard, but I was breathin' harder. Tink had a good workout, but it was quite a job for me to stay on. I needed a rest more than he did.

I had plenty of questions for Dewitt while we were restin' the horses. Questions like "How do you know when the horse has the critter you want?" Or "What do you watch, the cow or the horse?"

When the horses had rested, Dewitt went to cut another one. I did a better job of turnin' back this time and was even startin' to outguess Tink some. This was beginning to be more fun than I had expected.

When my turn come, Dewitt suggested the steer that I cut out. He thought this steer would be a little slower and I could learn more about cuttin' horses.

He was right, the steer was slower. But with Dewitt turning back, we made some pretty good pivots, turns and stops. The steer got a little faster and Tink almost missed him, but he headed him. As he was turning the steer, I heard a sudden squeal or a scream. It sounded like a mountain cat I'd heard scream before.

I pulled Tink up, "What in the world was that?"

"That's just ol' Tinker," says Dewitt. "He kinda likes that."

"Well, it scared me plum to death. I thought somebody got hurt," and wondered if it was me.

"No," says Dewitt grinnin', "Tink's just enjoyin' himself."

After a few more sessions, I come to learn a little more about cow cuttin' and ridin' cuttin' horses. I got to the point where I could keep Tink from cheatin' some when he'd let the fence turn one.

And I even got to the point where, when ol' Tink squealed his pleasure at headin' one, I could let out my own "Yahoo!" I was enjoyin' it too.

Wranglin' Dudes

There are lots of things that make a cowboy grow old: horse falls, buckin' horses, hard work and bad weather. Probably, though, the kind of work that ages a cowboy the fastest is wranglin' dudes.

A lot of cowboys, when they are between jobs, might pick up some work in town or try a little rodeoin' until the work starts again. While dudin' usually pays good and the work is generally pretty easy, a lot of fellers don't care much for it because of the way it ages a feller.

One time I was dudin' in Wyoming, on an outfit that run about a hundred head of horses. There was about six of us fellers working there and it was a company policy to usually send two or more wranglers on a ride—one to guide and one to ride alongside the dudes and remind them to keep a hold on their reins and not let their feet go all the way through the stirrups. Occasionally these "outriders" could help by picking up hats, cameras, scarves and other equipment dropped by the riders. Sometimes they could even help by picking up riders that dropped out of their saddles.

One time we had to pluck a youngster, about 10 years old, out of a tree. His horse had wandered around a tree the wrong way and under a limb. Instead of ducking, the kid put his hands up, took a hold of the limb and held on. The horse went on around the tree and back into line as nice as could be. It was such a peaceful event that nobody noticed the kid missing until we got another 40 yards up the trail and he hollered for someone to "come and get me." He was still hanging in the tree when one of the outriders got to him.

Sometimes, when going through a patch of willows, one of the kids' horses would walk off the trail right into the thickest part and scratch his belly. The kid would usually holler like he was being attacked by a bear, or worse—like he was hung up and being dragged. One of the outriders would have to go in and lead the horse out. This was usually pretty funny to everybody except the kid.

The way most of them kids could scream would age anyone. They would most always yell if they fell off, but if they saw a moose, deer, elk or even a squirrel or chipmunk, they'd scream. It gets pretty hard on a feller's nerves, knowing that any one of them screams could start the horses running. I've seen dudes fall off horses when the horses didn't do anything but stand still. And I've always had my doubts about dudes staying on when the horses was just walking.

We did have a stampede one time though. Somebody fell off their horse and as the horse trotted alongside the rest of the riders somebody yelled, "loose horse!" Then everybody was yellin' as the horses shifted gears and started to run. The outriders was pretty handy at riding alongside the kids, pullin' them off their horses and setting them on the ground.

A lot of folks got off their horses by themselves and a few fell off and one or two even got bucked off. When we made the final tally there was only the wranglers and one or two dudes still horseback.

We caught up what horses hadn't run home and started for home ourselves. Out of the 40-some-odd riders that had started out, only about five of the dudes rode back in. Luckily, nobody was hurt, but there was a lot of people complaining about having to walk back in.

The closer we got to the corrals, the more this bunch of people started lookin' like a bunch of cattle. All the cows was up in front and the calves and old bulls was making slow progress at the drag.

Everything turned out OK, for everyone except me, that is. Most of the kids wanted to go riding again, while most of their parents thought some relaxin' with a cold drink was in order. I was the one that needed the cold drink, but I had to take them kids out again. They all wanted to have as much fun as they did on the first ride, but all I could see was myself herdin' dudes back in.

Runaway

The team, Hap and Sally, weren't very well matched. Hap was a big rawboned bay horse that was always willing to work. Sometimes when we were short of kid horses, Hap would find himself saddled and packin' some kid around. He was mighty dependable.

Sally was just the opposite, ignorant, ornery and lazy. Somebody was always cussin' her out for somethin'.

On a dude outfit, a team and wagon can usually mean a lot of fun, but on this outfit the worst job a feller could get was driving the wagon. Not only because the team didn't work too well together but the wagon didn't give the best ride over the rough roads. The fact that a feller didn't get done at night 'til close to eleven o'clock didn't help matters much either. So, all the hands took turns drivin' the wagon so as nobody would get soured on it. Everybody was mighty pleased to have their turn at drivin' the wagon behind them.

One night I got Hap and Sally workin' together. It was my turn to drive the wagon and I thought I might get off easy since nobody had wanted to ride in the wagon. I was feelin' pretty good about it until the boss come up to me and told me to get Pete and hitch up the wagon 'cause some people just come in and wanted to ride.

Pete was in pretty good spirits as we caught up our saddle horses and rode the mile-and-a-half to the barn. We kept all the horses and equipment out of sight, off the road at night and trailed 'em back and forth mornings and evenings.

Pete's good spirits soon changed when we saw the harness. There's a right way to unharness a team and a lot of wrong ones. Whoever unharnessed the team had used one of the wrong ones. We finally got the harness straightened out after we had cussed everybody who could have messed up the harness and a lot of people who couldn't have. We finally got the team hitched and I says to Pete, "I'll drive 'em. We're running short of time and I'll make it up."

"OK," says Pete as he handed me the lines and climbed in. "I'll help you." With that, Pete took the end of the lines and whipped up Hap and Sally. They started right out at an easy lope. But Pete wasn't satisfied. "Sally, you old hussy, get up," he hollered, bringing the lines down on ol' Sally's rump again. The old horse really moved out this time. I'd never seen the ol' gal move so fast. And Hap, never one to be outdid, he was puttin' all he had into it.

The only thing wrong was that we wasn't on the road. We was tearin' off through the sagebrush. It didn't seem to bother Pete none. He whipped up Sally again.

By this time we was really movin', just a hummin' and a chuggin' through the brush. I was doin' all I could to miss the badger holes and rocks but wasn't having much success. Pete was still whippin' the horses and I was thinkin' we was havin' a runaway. I started to pull the team up and changed my mind. Now, I didn't think we was havin' a runaway, I knew we was!

We was comin' to the dirt road and I figured I could get the team stopped a little easier on the road rather than bouncin' through the sage-brush and over the rocks. But the shoulder of the road was soft and I couldn't get the right front wheel up on the road. We was skiddin' along with one wheel on the road and three wheels on the shoulder when Pete finally stopped encouragin' the horses.

"Stu," he hollers, "You better stop foolin' around and get this rig on the road before we hit that tree."

"Pete, I ain't foolin' around. I got about as much control over these horses as I got over the boss."

We was gettin' pretty close to the tree when we finally got the wagon on the road. Pete said the wheel only missed the tree by six inches and considerin' the hub stuck out another four inches, we didn't have much room to spare.

The horses was slowin' down some, but I still didn't have 'em going as slow as I wanted. We was gettin' close to where the pavement started and a hundred yards farther on was the parking lot.

We hit the pavement and somehow the horses managed to keep their balance. That pavement was pretty slick and with both horses being shod we was mighty lucky we didn't have a wreck there. We managed to make the turn into the parking lot but the wheels was makin' quite a screech as we did and headed to the office where the dudes was waitin'.

Horsin' Around A Lot   39

Pete jumped up and started wavin' his arms and hollerin' "Look out! Runaway! Look out!" People started scatterin' in every direction. I still didn't have the horses under 100 per cent control and they was still goin' pretty fast, but I was gettin' more control every minute. I couldn't get 'em stopped in front of the office so we kept on goin', took a turn around the building and I finally got the team stopped.

I was lookin' around to make sure nobody got hurt but I couldn't see anybody except the boss and he didn't look too happy. Pete jumped down, looked around and started to holler, "It's all right folks, you can come out now to admire the greatest stagecoach driver since Buffalo Bill!" He kept goin' on like that and pretty soon he had all the dudes around him believin' somethin' about a bear spookin' the horses and how the only thing that saved him was my skill as a driver. He had everybody believin' him except the boss. I could see he wasn't impressed as he started to walk toward me.

I was wonderin' if I should "volunteer" to roll up or wait for him to hand me my "walkin' papers" when a woman walks up to me.

"Do you always drive like that?" She asked.

"Yes mam," I says, hopin' to scare her off. I didn't like drivin' the wagon anyways and if I was goin' to get canned I sure didn't want to have to take it out.

"Good!" She says. "We came out here for some excitement on our vacation and this looks like the right place." She climbed in the wagon, followed by the rest of the dudes.

The boss didn't say nothin' except that I should "Make sure them folks get a SAFE ride!" That we did.

But Pete and me found ourselves hitchin' up the team and bringin' 'em up to the office a little more often—at a dead run. The boss said it was good for business.

My helper
'The Roper'

I guess I shouldn't say anything about anybody's ropin'. I'm about the worst there is. I can catch 'em sometimes, if I get enough throws, but usually my arm gets tired before I can latch onto somethin'. But as bad as my ropin' is, I know somebody who's worse at least I thought he was worse than me.

Art is an irrigator. During the spring, summer and fall, Art was pushin' the water over the 1,200 or so acres of irrigated land we had on the outfit in Idaho that I worked for not long ago. I was the cowboy. I guess I would have been a cowboss if there had been anybody to boss. But I had a bunch of old cows up there to graze some of the pasture land during the summer and they cleaned up the hay and grain fields in the fall and winter. I also got about 1,000 head of weaners every fall. We grew these heifers durin' the winter, bred 'em in the spring and sent 'em back to the home ranch in Utah.

My job was mostly takin' care of these heifers. We rode through 'em two or three times a day, lookin' for cattle sick or bloated or not doin' too well. Those that needed some doctorin' or some help were brought into the sick pen or recovery pen, given what help we could give 'em, and watched pretty close for a couple of days.

When these heifers arrived in the late fall, I usually got one of the farm hands to give me some help. Most of the fellers I had to help me didn't know much about cattle, especially sick cattle, but they seemed willin' to learn and more than willin' to saddle up a horse and play "cowboy" for a while. Of course they didn't realize that them long hours in the saddle can make a feller pretty tired at night. And there ain't no heaters built on saddles for them cold days. So, most of the time I found myself pullin' sick cattle from the pens while my tired and shiverin' companion opened the gate.

Last fall I did have some help and I thought the feller might become a pretty fair cowboy some day. But when it started gettin' cold, he thought a warmer climate might be more to his liking, so he packs up his gear and moves out. That's how I come to get Art.

After the pumps was turned off, Art didn't have much to do. He kinda wandered around tryin' to help where he could, but mostly gettin' in the way. So, when the would-be-cowboy left, the superintendent comes up to me and says, "Stu, seein' as you're short of help, why don't you take Art and let him help you? I don't know how much help he'll be, but maybe he can help you 'til we can get somebody else."

From the look in his eyes and the tone of his voice, I knew this was more than a favor, it was more like a command.

The next mornin', Art was waitin' in the tack room when I showed up. "The 'super' says you want me to help you for awhile. What saddle do you want me to use?" I showed him a company rig that wasn't being used, gave him a couple of blankets and a bridle and showed him his horse when we got to the catch pen.

He wasn't too pleased with his horse when I pointed him out. He said he'd rather ride the palomino, the one he'd seen the 'super' ridin'.

"No," I says, "That's the superintendent's private horse. You better take the sorrel I showed you, ol' Donde. You can get the work done on him."

Reluctantly, Art went and caught the sorrel. "Just like the others," I thought. "Wanna ride the colorful horse in the bunch and don't much care about gettin' the job done." Even worse, he didn't know the in's and out's of the bridle. I had to bridle his horse for him.

I caught up my own horse, saddled him and was leadin' him past where Art was still saddlin' his horse. He was havin' problems.

His back cinch was done up, but he was havin' some trouble with his front cinch. There wasn't a tackaberry on the latigos or a tongue on the cinch, so a knot had to be tied. I showed him how and we was ready to start work.

As I watched Art climb on his horse, I was thinkin' that I'd done more for dudes on the dude outfits I'd worked on. Now I was doin' it for a feller that was supposed to help me cowboy!

Art wasn't much help. He didn't know anything about cattle or sick cattle and most of the time he was in the way. Most of the time, but not all the time, because he was learnin'.

He learnt not to press the cattle too much, and where to be, sometimes, anyways. But occasionally he'd get in the wrong spot, not 'cause his horse did, but 'cause he got to thinkin' sometimes that he knowed more than the horse did. But he didn't. As far as help goes, I'd have been better off if I'd have just taken ol' Donde in the pens with me and let Art set in the bunkhouse.

But Art did come in mighty handy. Sometimes he'd booger those cattle so bad I'd have to rope 'em to get 'em out. I sorta looked on this as a blessin' since I love to rope. But I ain't no good, and every chance I get to practice I figure is helpin' me out.

As it come about, Art spooked this one particular animal away from the gate a couple of times and I got so mad that I jerked my rope down, made a loop and proceeded to rope that animal, stretch her neck a little and put her out of that pen. But I missed my first loop, and the second, too.

I started to pull my horse up to make another loop. I'd made the second loop and run but I pulled up now, figurin' that runnin' that heifer around would do her more harm than I could do her in the sick pen. "Yep," I thought, as I pulled my horse in, "Better let that heifer go for now and come back and get her later when she ain't so excited."

But Art had some different ideas. He knew I wanted that heifer out of the pen and he had his rope down. As I was pullin' up he came foggin' by me, kickin' his horse every jump.

How he stayed on his horse, I don't know, but he came a chuggin' by me ridin' mighty loose, and swingin' a mighty big loop.

I'd seen Art take his rope down before and I knew he hadn't had much to do with one. When he'd taken his rope down it looked like he was only makin' half the effort to catch something. From the size of his loop before, he couldn't have caught more than a Mason jar, and from the way he throwed it he didn't want to catch more than that.

But he wanted to catch this one—he wanted to catch her mighty bad.

His loop was big enough to catch four or five head and the way he was movin' that horse on, if he'd have had spurs he wouldn't have got him stopped by now.

He was swingin' his loop so fast it's a wonder he didn't go straight up in the air, like a helicopter. But when he finally let 'er fly, the loop was true and it settled over the heifer's head slick as a whistle.

There was only one problem. This was the first animal Art had ever roped. After he roped her he didn't know what to do!

I could see that the heifer was gettin' farther away from the roper when she should have been stayin' closer. And I could see that the rider was gettin' farther away from the saddle when he should be sittin' closer.

As things come about, Art couldn't find the saddle horn, or he didn't know what it was for, but he wouldn't let go of the rope 'til he hit the ground.

I caught up Art's horse, then picked up Art. He wasn't hurt, but he was mighty happy nobody else had seen. I had to get Art's rope off and still get the heifer into the sick pen.

As it turned out, gettin' the heifer into the sick pen wasn't hard. Gettin' Art's rope off was.

I took my rope down again. I figured the best way to get Art's rope was to rope the heifer by the hind feet, then Art could slip up and get the rope off.

But the heifer wouldn't cooperate. I slipped up behind her and set a real nice heel trap. But the heifer wouldn't step into it. She wouldn't even kick at it.

Undaunted, I coiled the rope and threw another heel trap. It was a mighty nice throw and that loop set up perfect. It laid back against the heifer's inside hocks as pretty as could be. But she still wouldn't step into it.

I says to Art, "Get off your horse and twist her tail and make her move into that loop!"

Art got off his horse, moved the heifer into the loop, I jerked the slack and she was caught, even though she didn't resist much. Art got his rope off and I give the heifer some medicine and we turned her loose.

The next day, as we moved into the pen, Art took his rope down when he seen the heifer. He was tryin' to better his average, but I stopped him.

"No," I says, "She was in better shape before we doctored her yesterday. Better leave her alone." Reluctantly, the roper hung up his rope.

Lightning
A cowboy never knows when it will strike

I've heard a lot of fellers brag about how they ain't scared of a thing, man or beast. I guess there's some people around like that, but I ain't one of 'em. I've been in a few situations with man an' beast that I'd sure hate to have to live over an' try an' come out as good as I did. But there is three things I don't mind admittin' to bein' scared of—women, water and lightning.

Women, I'm learnin' to handle. After eight years of marriage an' three kids, I'm gettin' over bein' scared of girls.

Water still causes me some problems. I don't mind drinkin' it, an' I don't mind bathin' in it. What I do mind is gettin' in it over my head. To tell the truth, I can't swim the length of a bathtub. The only reason I get in one is cause I can keep a good hold on the soap dish an' keep from goin' under. I get along with water just fine as long as I don't get in it too deep.

I can hide from women an' keep from goin' in the water, but I never know when lightnin's goin' to strike. I've heard too many stories about cowboys takin' off spurs, bits an' belt buckles durin' a thunderstorm, to give me any confidence about goin' outside durin' a thunderstorm. There's too many bleached bones of some critter that got hit by lightnin' up on top of barren ridges an' plenty of split trees in the forest. No, lightnin' ain't nothin' to be fooled with.

I was guidin' a trail ride with about 10 dudes up in the Grand Teton National Park in Wyoming when a thundershower come up real sudden. We'd passed the halfway point an' all we could do was try an' get back as fast as we could. Because we had some inexperienced riders with us, we couldn't hit a steady trot an' make it back a little faster without endangerin' the welfare of the less experienced. Consequently, we hurried up, then slowed down when some of the dudes got to hangin' out too far from their saddles.

Don't think I wasn't havin' some problems, keepin' an eye on the dudes an' tryin' to watch out for lightnin'. Seems like every time lightnin' would hit pretty close, an' at times it seemed like it was only an arms length away when it struck, we'd hurry up to get away from it.

But we couldn't hurry too fast 'cause of the inexperienced riders, an' I'd also heard somewhere that a hot horse draws lightnin' to him; probably an old wives tale, but I didn't want to test it out. We had to take our time. I didn't want no dudes fallin' off an' I didn't want to be drawin' no lightnin'.

Needless to say, we made it back without anybody gettin' hit by lightnin' or fallin' off. But I still don't put any trust in lightnin'.

A couple of years later, I was struck by lightnin'. Well, not struck, but

I had a shockin' experience. I was workin' at a feedlot that had a 20,000 head capacity an' all these cattle was kept in pens made out of pipe an' cable fencing.

I was out one evenin' checkin' the cattle before callin' it a day. I'd noticed a storm buildin' up earlier in the day, but hadn't given it much thought, figurin' I could finish up an' be done before the storm hit.

I was gettin' cattle out of pens that was fat, an' ready to slaughter. I had a bunch in the alley an' was just about ready to call it quits when the storm hit. The rain really come down an' it don't take much rain in a feedlot to make things real slick fast! I decided I'd put the cattle away that I had an' call it a day.

As I was pushin' the steers up the alley, I noticed a steer that was bloated. Now he wasn't bloated enough to stick, but if he stayed in the pen overnight an' had as much water as he wanted, he'd probably be dead in the morning.

I figured I'd put him in the alley overnight an' put him back where he belonged in the mornin'. It wouldn't be overly rough, the steer was right next to the gate an' it wouldn't take much to open it, ease him out, close the gate an' leave him.

For once, everything worked out like I'd planned. It couldn't have worked out nicer, except that it was rainin'. I got through gettin' the steer out, an' was real pleased with myself for havin' done it so easy.

I reached down to latch the gate closed an' when my hand was 'bout a half an inch away from the latch, there was a "pop" an' a blue spark an' I felt a slight shock. My horse, Partner, felt the shock too, and shied away. I bumped the gate as I was tryin' to get back in the saddle an' moved it enough to close it and lock it.

It didn't take me long to figure out that lightnin' had struck somewhere along that pipe an' cable fence, an' I didn't take long to wonder about it! I put the cattle I had in an empty pen after cuttin' back the bloated steer and headed for the barn. I wasn't goin' to stay out there an' give lightnin' a chance to strike twice!

Horsin' Around A Lot   45

Buckaroo

I was workin' out in Nevada on a good cow outfit with some real good hands and a good string of horses. There was about ten of us buckaroos, counting the reps from other outfits.

We was out on the wagon, branding a lot of good-looking, husky calves and scattering the cows over the range, so as to get the best use of the grass and still have good grass the next year, and for the years to come.

Of course, scattering the cows meant we had to scatter the bulls where the cows was so as they'd be enough calves to stay in business the next year.

All we needed was an extra hand or two and we'd have been in good shape. Our horses were staying in pretty good shape, but that didn't mean the hands weren't getting kinda tired. The horses in the cavy was only used about once a week but the buckaroos was going every day.

There was plenty of hands before we went on the wagon, but one feller bucked off his horse, hurt something in his back, and even though he could get around some, the doc's orders kept ole John from riding. A couple of other fellers decided they couldn't stay away from town for a few months, so they rolled up. We was kinda short handed, but we went on the wagon anyway. When there's work to be done with cattle, it don't wait til there are enough hands.

But it really wasn't too bad. We usually got back to camp in time to have a game of cards. Now cards in this cow camp wasn't like a person might expect from watching television westerns. We played Hearts.

There was a lot riding on this game of Hearts. Me and Harry Taylor was teamed up against the cowboss and Will. We kept track of which team won the most games every night and it was entered in the cowboss' tally book. The team that had won the most games by the time we left the wagon and went to the home ranch had to help the losers drink a six pack of beer or soda pop. This depends on who won or lost.

This was mighty important to both teams cause if Harry and me won, that would mean the cowboss and Will would have to buy some beer and help us drink it. This prospect was mighty pleasing to Harry and me, we sorta liked a cold beer or two every now and then. But Will and the cowboss didn't much care for beer; they'd rather have soda pop. Me and Harry would rather have beer. So the games took on an added excitement every night.

Harry and me, we worked out some signals so as we could let each other know what cards we had, and when the cowboss and Will found out, they worked out their own signals. Things finally got to the point where there was signals and counter-signals and counter-counter-signals.

Every time Harry and me saw the cowboss and Will riding together, we figured they'd caught on to our signals, so we changed them. But there was one night when our card playing was disrupted. The cowboss had to take a feller to the home ranch and Harry and me had to change our signals.

This feller the cowboss had to take to town had showed up sorta sudden and his departure was kinda sudden, too. It all started when we was coming back to camp one afternoon. About a hundred yards away from camp we all noticed the company pickup parked in front of the cook shack. Figuring someone had brought some supplies and the mail, we started a horse race for camp. Kinda foolish for growed men, but then the last part of cowboy is "boy".

When we pulled our horses up in front of the cook shack and got done seeing who left the longest slide marks, I noticed a new hand leaning against the railing. He looked like a cowboy, but when I was unsaddling my horse and he was walking towards me, he didn't walk like a cowboy. He asked me if I was the cowboss. "Nope," I says, "that's him over there, turning loose the bay horse."

I couldn't figure how come this new feller mistook me for the cowboss cause he's a pretty big feller and I'm kinda a puny little guy. Then I got to thinking maybe my horse had slid the farthest and left the best slide marks. I went back to check, but he hadn't.

The new feller was hired and the card game went on same as usual that night. The next morning, most everybody was interested in seeing what kind of horse and what horse in particular the cowboss would call out for the new hand. When he roped a gray horse for the new feller, I figured there wouldn't be any action that morning. I'd had the gray horse, Steel, in my string at one time but traded him for another horse. Even though some of the hands said Steel could really buck, he'd never bucked with me and I figured him for a pretty dependable horse.

As I was untracking my horse and trying to figure out how he got his name, Trapeez, I heard the unmistakable sounds of a cowboy getting bucked off–hooves tearing up the ground, leather creaking, the thud of a body hitting the ground, a couple of cuss words and stirrups popping over an empty saddle.

I knew these sounds pretty well, I'd been throwed before, too; there ain't a cowboy that hasn't.

I turned to see who got dusted and it was the newcomer. Steel had bucked him off, but he was on his feet almost as fast as he'd been bucked off and was trying to catch Steel. He got the horse caught an' got right back on, and was promptly helped, by the horse, off. Third time is a charm and when he got on the horse again, Steel didn't even buck, so we started out.

Now when you start out to gather cattle on most Nevada cow outfits, you start out at a trot and keep it up for a good many miles. The horses are tough, and many times prove to be tougher than the riders. This was the newcomer's problem. The longer we trotted, the farther behind he fell. When we got to where the cowboss started scattering riders, he still hadn't showed up. We figured he'd went back to camp and started gathering cattle.

We held a branding that day, on a well used "rodere" (Spanish word that means to hold) ground. We had a lot of cattle with calves needing brands and was about half done when here comes the newcomer.

I was holding the cattle, along with four or five other buckaroos, while a couple of fellers heeled the calves and drug them up to the fire where they was branded, vaccinated, earmarked and castrated if necessary.

I hadn't even seen the newcomer coming in and was startled when he rode up beside me and said, "Whew! Thought I'd never find you guys."

"We been here quite a while," I says.

"Where'd you find all them cows? You know, riding out here, I never saw a cow until I got here."

"Sometimes they hide," I says, "under rocks and leaves and fallen tree twigs."

"They sure are hard to find," he said.

"Yep."

Pretty soon the cowboss calls me and Harry to go in and take a turn at heeling some calves. As I was dragging my calf up to the fire, the cowboss says, "What did the dude say when he rode up, Stu?"

"He said he'd met a fairy princess on the way and they went on a picnic."

"From the likes of him, I wouldn't doubt it."

"Well, he did ask me where we found all these cows."

"What did you tell him?"

I told him we found them under rocks. Isn't that where they live?"

"Yep," said the cowboss, grinning, "that's where they live. They need a place to get in out of the rain, when it rains."

I went out to catch another calf, and after a few throws, I did. As I went past the cowboss, dragging the calf to the fire, I says, "Why don't you let the new feller rope a few?"

"I think you need the practice. If he can't rope any better than you, we'll still be here all night."

"Maybe so. But there's still about three calves in there that ain't branded."

"Still might take us all night if you don't quit jawing and catch one every now and then."

It wasn't long before the last calf had been branded and we was sitting around, waiting for the cowboss to finish counting ears for his tally before we started home. Harry and me was kinda anxious to get back to camp. We'd worked out some new signals for the card game and was anxious to try them out.

We started back to camp at a trot and it wasn't long before we'd left the newcomer behind again. Nobody was worried. The horse would bring him back to camp. But when we got to camp, turned our horses loose, got some supper and maybe a little nap, a few of the fellers did mention that the newcomer could have fallen off his horse or something. But the cowboss figured he was alright, cause if the horse was loose, he'd have been home by now.

We'd been in camp about three hours and the sun was just going behind the west mountains when the newcomer showed up. He was riding Steel, but from the dust on his boots, we figured he'd probably walked a right good part of the way back to camp.

The cowboss had put the new hand's bedroll in the truck and told the newcomer to put his saddle in, too. "You ain't no cowboy," he said. "Maybe they can use you on the farm."

As they drove away, Will said that the cowboss was right, he wasn't no cowboy.

"Probably didn't even know how to play hearts, either," muttered Harry.

Rustler !

Back in the old days, I guess a feller could get in a lot of trouble branding his neighbor's stock with his own iron. From what the old-timers tell me, when a feller was caught red-handed, if he wasn't shot trying to get away, the punishment was administered on the range, with a rope that needed stretching and a stout tree limb acting as executioners. I'd guess that when a feller was starting his own herd in them days, he had to be mighty careful.

There was a time, about seven or eight years ago, when I wasn't so careful and mighty glad there wasn't any stout tree limbs around. I sure had everybody mad at me. Now don't get me wrong, I didn't have no intentions of starting a herd by borrowing the neighbors cattle and I ain't gonna tell you that the neighbor's calf run into my loop while I was laying a trap for another calf. No sir. All I did was rope a calf and drag it up to the fire… twice.

I was out in Nevada, buckarooing on a pretty big outfit, the name of which I ain't gonna mention 'cause there still might be some hard feelings over this incident. We were out on the "wagon", branding calves. We'd been out for about a month and I figured we'd have about a month and a half more. The pay was pretty good considering room and board was throwed in. The "room" was a tent, which wasn't so bad unless you spread your bedroll out under a hole in the roof and it rained. The board more than made up for any inconvenience. That old cook must have thought us buckaroos was kings.

I've eaten in a lot of cow camps and the fare was mostly the same: meat, taters, biscuits and coffee. There is nothing wrong with that at all. That's "stick to your ribs" kind of grub. But when the cook found out how we all liked our steaks, they was fixed that way. Even the roasts was cooked so as everyone got meat the way he wanted it, from "burnt" to "warm, but still kicking".

What got everybody, though, was the desserts. I hadn't had till then, and ain't had since, a doughnut or a piece of cake or pie in a cow camp. But we had 'em all we wanted. That cook sure took care of us and we took care of him. He always had plenty of water and plenty of wood and always a volunteer to help with the dishes. Nobody in a cow camp wants the title of "cook's flunky", but in that cow camp that year everybody had a turn at washing or drying dishes. Not 'cause they had to but 'cause they wanted to. "Cookie" worked over a wood-burning stove for 12 or 14 of us. If I could rope as good as he could cook but that's where I got in trouble, with my roping.

We was holding a rodeo, branding the slicks. It was my turn to rope and I figured I wasn't doing too bad. I was catching one every time the other ropers caught one, but it was taking me more loops.

I roped one calf, drug him up to the fire and was watching the cowboss starting to earmark him when he says, "Let him go, Stu. He's the neighbor's calf."

I let the calf go and says to the cowboss that I never noticed an earmark or brand on the calf. And the cowboss said that while the calf wasn't branded or earmarked, he had the neighbor's wattle under the chin, not a very good wattle, but it was still there.

We were just about finished for the day and I was started back to the fire where the cowboss would count the ears and write down how many we branded that day in the tally book. Then I saw a calf that didn't have a brand where there should have been one.

My loop was still ready, so I put it on him and dallied up. Some how or another my rope got tangled between the horse's hind legs and he started to pitch some as we drug the calf to the fire. The fellers working on the ground held the calf while I calmed the horse down, stepped over the rope and held the calf while they branded, castrated, vaccinated and earmarked the calf.

As somebody went to wattle the calf, he said, "Hey, this is the neighbor's calf."

The ground crew stopped what they was doing and went to investigate. I saw the heads nod as somebody pointed out the neighbor's wattle, under the chin. The same calf I had roped before and had to let go.

Somebody walked past me and said, "Stu, you just rustled the neighbor's calf for us."

"Not me," I said, trying to be funny. "You guys branded him." As it turned out it wasn't very funny.

"Is that the only calf you can catch?" somebody asked.

"Nobody else could catch him," I answered. I was still trying to be funny.

"Turn him loose," says the cowboss.

"Don't you want to vent the brand or something?" I asked.

"No. We'll just give the neighbor a check in the fall for the calf, though he won't like it."

I sure didn't feel good about it till we got back to camp. I sure did justice to the cook's dinner and the chocolate cake and was doubly pleased that nobody did range justice to me particularly the rightful owners of that calf.

Christmas Joy

Last Christmas, the most practical gift I received was a pair of long johns. This set of winter underwear was regular "old time" style, one piece, from neck to toe with buttons up the front and back.

This was a regular "union suit"; the first I had seen for years. In fact, I thought they had stopped making them. This was just what a skinny old cowboy, like myself, needed to keep warm during the winter.

I'd looked around in town for this particular kind of underwear but didn't see any and was too embarrassed to ask. So I usually ended up buying two-piece underwear for the winter. This was really unfortunate because a cowboy does a lot of physical work and the top part of the two-piece underwear would become untucked from my jeans, thereby creating a draft up my back and down what was left of my back to my lower extremities.

Needless to say, I was mighty pleased with this gift and sorta' anxious to try it on, but gave up on the idea of trying it on right away because, as I held it up in front of me for everyone to see, some of the neighbors wanted me to put it on and give them a fashion show. I declined for two reasons, namely, I don't usually go parading around at Christmas parties in my union suit and, when a feller tries something like this on for the first time, he can't always be sure which buttons are buttoned and which aren't.

When I finally tried it on, in private, it did fit.

I went back to work the next day, wearing my new union suit, under my regular work clothes, of course, and felt mightly comfortable minus the drafts up and down my back that I had felt wearing the two-piece outfits.

I was riding along with Jerry and Blair, real pleased with my new suit, and couldn't help mentioning, "How are you guys doing for warmth?"

"We're freezing to death," said Jerry.

"You should have asked Santa for a union suit like I have," I said. "They really is warm and comfortable."

"If they are really that warm, then you can open that wire gate ahead of us. It is just too cold for Jerry and me to get off our horses and do it, and besides, I think I'm froze to this saddle," said Blair.

"Okay," says I, "but you fellers really ought to do it. Moving around would make you warmer and I'm so warm now that I might work up such a sweat openin' and closin' that gate that I'd catch pneumonia and die!"

"That would be a blessing," said Jerry. "If you did die, we wouldn't have to listen to you tellin' us about your union suit an' how warm it is."

When we got to the gate, I opened it. But getting back on my horse was a job. With my union suit, chaps and a heavy winter coat on, I was having trouble reaching my foot into the stirrup. Every time I got my foot into the stirrup, it would slip out.

Jerry and Blair were both enjoying the "show" and Blair remarked, "Stu must be gettin' old. He can't even get his foot in the stirrup."

"No. It ain't that. It is just that there is some ice on my stirrup and with the snow on my boot, I keep slippin' out. My union suit don't help either."

"Look at that," said Blair. "His underwear don't want him to work."

"That is why they call it a 'union suit'," said Jerry.

"You boys could stop jawing and give me a hand."

"What's the matter? One of your buttons come undone?"

"No, but every time I raise my leg to put my foot in the stirrup, my union suit pulls on my shoulder, makin' it harder for me to raise my foot."

"Well, I'll help you get in the saddle," said Jerry as he pulled my coat, shirt, union suit and me into the saddle, "but you'll have to button your own buttons!"

The Makins' Of A Good Horse

At one dude outfit I worked on, they didn't own any horses. They leased them from a horse trader up around Riverton, Wyoming. Most years they'd get the same horses back in the spring, but there'd be some new ones to replace the older horses or them that didn't work out too good the year before.

It was mighty interestin' to watch 'em unload the horses in the spring. Most everybody was lookin' for familiar faces, them good old horses that was dependable or maybe a favorite that was a hand's guide horse. 'Course there was always some new horses, all sizes, shapes and colors.

Now, these new horses always drawed attention from the hands. They came from wherever the horse trader could get 'em. Some of 'em carried brands and some was slick. There was a few with some pretty mean scars, like they'd tangled with some wire at one time or another. Judgin' from the brands on some, they'd traded hands a few times.

'Course all these horses had to be tried out. We couldn't be puttin' a dude on some old rodeo horse that had quit buckin' hard enough to throw off good bronc riders, but hadn't quit buckin' hard enough. We got a few of these horses that hadn't forgot all they knowed, and sometimes toppin' off these horses got to be kinda lively. 'Course horses that did a good job of buckin' was returned to the horse trader unless one of the fellas wanted a practice horse to sharpen up on.

There was one truck load of horses come in that I sure won't forget. Most of 'em was proven dude horses: ol' Buck, the big buckskin gelding that was the best kid horse on the outfit; Jupiter and Jennifer, a matched pair of greys that were 'pert' near inseparable; Slim, a big sorrel Thoroughbred kind of horse; and a couple more. There was some new horses too. Of the new horses I remember best on this load was Spud, an older bay gelding, and Pecos, a buckskin. These two horses had the same brands on them. There was two other horses that had the same brands, although they was different from what Spud and Pecos packed. They were mares, called Henrietta and One Spot. Henrietta and One Spot come off the same outfit and they even had the same kinda build.

Spud and Pecos turned out to be mighty good horses even though they both had some age on 'em. Even with the age, they was still mighty quick. Most dudes kick a horse to get him goin', but Spud and Pecos had been rode by some mighty good hands where they come from; and a kick to the ribs on either horse usually resulted in more than the dude anticipated. So they became guide horses and somebody who appreciated a good horse got to use 'em, rather than a dude tryin' to be a cowboy.

The remark was made by more than one hand that it took a mighty good hand to ride either one when they was younger, and it took a mighty good hand to put the kind of rein on 'em that they had. The outfit they come from was known for good horses.

Henrietta and One Spot was different. There was some misgivings as to how good they might be, right from the start.

The start come on the next morning when we was saddlin' up. We hadn't had time to try out the new horses the day they arrived, so each one of the hands was instructed to "throw your saddle on this horse." We saddled in a chute so as we could speed up the operation some. It would have taken time to catch, lead in and saddle 80 or 100 head of horses each day, so we had a chute where we could saddle six or eight head at a time. It was pot luck. We'd figured it up. Walt would get the first, Ron the second, I'd get the third and Pete would get the fourth. I guess the boss had sized up the rest of the horses 'cause he said he'd top 'em off.

As it turned out, Walt got Spud and Ron got Pecos. While the rest of us was saddlin' the other horses, they tried their's out and both come back with big grins on their faces. They was mighty pleased. They'd got some good horses.

The next new horse to come through was One Spot, and I found myself puttin' my saddle on her. She was a buckskin, sorta crossed between a true buckskin and a sorrel. She had a white stripe down her face and four white socks. She got her name from a big white spot, about a foot and a half across, on her left hip. I'd have called her Two Spot, 'cause she had some white on her belly, on the right side.

I got the saddle screwed on all right and went to saddle another horse. When the horses in the chute was saddled, somebody pulled the pole and let 'em out. Normally, nobody paid no attention to the horses leaving, but I stopped a moment to watch One Spot and try to figure out if she'd be OK or not. I wasn't alone, because as soon as One Spot got some room, she really fired. The sound of empty stirrups poppin' over the saddle drawed everybody's attention. The way that horse was buckin' made me feel sorta grateful that I wasn't in the saddle and sorta fearful knowin' that I soon would be.

When she stopped buckin', nobody said anything but Pete. "Sure bucks good, don't she, Stu?"

"Yep" was all I could manage. She had bucked good. Better than good, and I was havin' my doubts as to being able to stay on her if she did somethin' like that while I was on her.

"Looks like some of them dudes might get a show this morning," says Pete. The new horses would be used today, regardless.

"Yep," I says. "They might get two!"

Pete didn't say nothin' but went to saddlin' up. He didn't notice it but his saddle was put on Henrietta. When the other horses was saddled, the pole was pulled and the sound of stirrup leathers poppin' was heard again.

"What horse is that?" asked Pete.

"Yours," I answered cheerfully. "You might notice she's got the same brand as the one I drawed."

"Oh," says Pete as his eyes bugged out.

"Looks like them dudes might get a show this morning," I said. "Yep," answered Pete. Pete wasn't talkin' much as we finished saddlin' and neither was I. We both had the prospect of tryin' out some horses that didn't look too good to start with.

We got the rest of the horses saddled and was catchin' up our saddle horses to jingle up the horses to the day corrals and office.

I noticed Pete catching up a good old dependable dude horse to jingle the horses up to the day corrals, just as I was doin'. "Why ain't you ridin' the horse your saddle is on?" I asked.

"She's a little hard to catch," he answered. "Besides, we're kinda in a rush this morning."

"Yep," I says as I climbed aboard Renegade, a good, gentle dude horse.

The other fellers was lightin' up smokes, figurin' on maybe watchin' a bronc ride, but Pete and me was figurin' on the same thing – don't ride one of them broncs while chasin' a bunch of horses through the pines. A feller might get in trouble doin' that, and Pete and me figured there was plenty of time for gettin' in trouble later.

There was dudes lined up at the day corral when we run the horses in. The boss was all business. "Get them people mounted up and let's get this first ride taken care of!"

There wasn't much time for Pete and me to contemplate how our horses was goin' to be, but we took time. We found ourselves comparin' notes on the two horses every time we could.

"Do you think that Henrietta horse will buck as hard with me on her as she did this morning?" Pete asked.

"I don't know, Pete," I says. "Them horses was bound to get tired running up here. Maybe they're tuckered out by now."

"I dunno. The bay mare's got a bad look in her eye," says Pete.

"But she sure didn't buck as hard as mine," I says.

"I don't know," says Pete. "Both bucked pretty hard. They come from the same outfit. The top hand on that outfit probably had a time with 'em or they wouldn't be here."

I was gonna answer, but the boss come up and tells us that we'd better stop jawin' and get to work.

Pete and me had been talkin' and we didn't notice the ride was ready to go. As a matter of fact, everybody was mounted and started off. The next thing that was to happen was toppin' off our horses.

The boss asked me if I was ready to top off this mare, One Spot. "No," I says, "I got a little adjustment in my rig to make first." He asked Pete, and Pete found some excuse so the boss figured he'd try out Buck, the kids' horse, while we was makin' our adjustments.

My adjustment consisted of takin' off a lead rope I had coiled on my saddle. I found this lead rope mighty convenient for leadin' in unruly riders – the horses didn't usually give no trouble. As I was takin' off this lead rope and the boss was preparin' to get on Buck, Walt climbs the corral next to me, watchin' what's goin' on.

"See the foreman is goin' to top off Buck," says Walt.

"Yep," I says. "Don't think anything will come of it, though."

"Nope," he says. "Last year some kid fell off him, was hollerin' and screamin' like he'd been kilt, but old Buck just starts munchin' on grass even though this kid is screamin' bloody murder. He starts grazin', just like it happened every day. I don't think you could get that horse to buck if you promised him a garbage can full of oats every day!"

"That's sure nice to know, Walt, but right now Pete and me is concerned about what we're goin' to be forkin' next."

"I know Pete's concerned," Walt says, "and you probably are too, but…"

"Stu! You ought to have had enough time to make any changes in your rig. Get on that horse and ride it! " The boss interrupted us, makin' a show for some of the dudes that had gathered.

I led the horse to the center of the corral. I was mighty careful to check the rig, the cinchas, the stirrups, and even the saddle strings. I checked everything twice. I finally ran out of things to check. The time had come to climb aboard. There wasn't anything else to do.

Now, I don't mind gettin' bucked off so much, but I really don't appreciate a crowd watchin' when it happens. But it was do or die right now. The boss was circulatin' through the crowd, spreadin' rumors about 'a horse what ain't been rode and a cowboy what ain't been throwed', and here I was steppin' up on this horse.

I was mighty careful to climb aboard. I got myself set in the saddle as best I could and let the mare's head loose. I watched her head, her ears, but there was no movement. I strained to feel the slightest movement a muscle twitch, a nerve–but nothin' came. So I coaxed her a little bit and we moved around the corral in a smooth trot. Then a smooth lope. I spurred her a little. There was no reaction–at least not what the dudes wanted. I tested the horse some, and there wasn't any buck in her. As a matter of fact, she turned out to be a different kind of horse.

Henrietta didn't buck either. As a matter of fact, them four horses turned out to be the best in the bunch. Maybe the old sayin' about a horse that ain't got no fight at first ain't worth anything is true.

As it ended up, Walt and me shared Spud on this dude outfit, Spud being the best at the time. Consequently, Spud got to feelin' pretty good, and when a special occasion arose, Walt and me had to draw straws to see who rode him. Pecos was in my string and Walt's, too. Them two horses was special occasion horses on a dude outfit and got a lot of the good work.

Henrietta became Walt's wife's horse and One Spot, she became a kid pony. Good horse that she was, she became the best kid horse on the place. I sure wouldn't have believed it from the way I first felt about forkin' her the first time.

Just A Kid's Horse

I was sittin' over a cup of coffee out in Nevada, out of a job and wonderin' what I'd do next. The outfit I was workin' on let all their buckaroos go, promisin' us a job when the fall gather started. In the meantime, the cowboss would do what little ridin' was necessary, scatterin' some salt an' doctorin' them cattle what needed it. He'd also have his kids to help when needed.

I didn't have anything to worry about. I had a couple of months wages in my pocket. It wouldn't be enough to live on but I could get by on it.

I'd been over to the saddle shop and picked up some things that I needed. While I was there, I mentioned to the owner that the hands on our outfit had been laid off for a couple of months. I told him I didn't know what I'd do but I'd be back for the fall gather.

Now I was orderin' my second cup of coffee, thinkin' maybe I could take a small vacation and see some of the country I'd never seen before. I was just beginnin' to wonder what sleepin' in might be like when the owner of the saddle shop come bustin' in.

"Stu, I been lookin' all over for you. Got a job for you if you want it," he told me. "A feller come in right after you left and asked if I knew somebody who could help brand some late calves and move some cattle around. The job only lasts a month or so, but he's got to have a man tomorrow."

I wrote down the man's name, found out where I could most likely find him, finished my coffee and set out to talk to him about the job.

When I found him he was just sittin' down to supper in another cafe. I got the job but missed out on the meal. I figured I could get supper at the ranch, but I had some 60-odd miles to go first. Everything I owned in the world – a saddle, a few bridles, my bedroll and some extra clothes was in my car, so all I had to do was drive. I made it to the ranch by suppertime and the grub was better than any I could have got in town.

There was only two other hands, plus the cook. All three was oldtimers, more than likely pensioners, and I figured the only reason an extra hand was needed was to do the heavy work like wrasslin' the calves and maybe use the horses that might be a little rank or spook easy.

Next mornin' I was up at 4:30, ready to hit the saddle. The other two old waddies wasn't up yet, but things was stirrin' in the cook shack, so I went over for some coffee.

"You're up mighty early, sonny," says the cook. I didn't take kindly to the "sonny", but I always figured it was best to be mighty courteous to cooks.

"Yes sir," I says, "a feller can't make a living in bed."

"Well, around here things don't happen 'til the boss comes out of the big house, usually sometime around eight. Boy, you got three hours of nothin' to do," the cook says.

"I was sorta plannin' on takin' a vacation when I took this job, so maybe I can get a paid vacation," I added.

"There really ain't much work here, so enjoy it while you can."

I got to watchin' the cook and he reminded me of the oldtime cooks everybody talks about. Sorta grumpy, sayin' just what he pleases to whoever he wanted. He always had a homemade smoke in his mouth and it seemed like an ash was ever ready to fall into whatever he was fixin'.

On this outfit, I sorta figured I'd be gettin' some rough horses to ride. But that first day, much to my surprise, I got a pretty fair horse. I even got to thinking that this might be a pretty fair vacation–all the horses on the place was about the same.

The next mornin' the boss points out a horse to me he calls "Twinkle". I figured this was sort of a strange name for a horse, particularly on a Nevada cow outfit. I guess the boss seen a funny look on my face, 'cause he started to say somethin' about how the kids rode him all last summer.

I was wonderin' what kinda kids this feller had when I noticed how the horse was eyeballin' me while I saddled him. I also noticed the two oldtimers watchin'. I didn't know what to think. The horse had a hump in his back, the oldtimers was kinda interested, and even though I hadn't figured out the horse, I was startin' to suspect things.

I took off the hobbles, untracked the horse, cheeked him and climbed aboard, expectin' the worst. I turned the cheek strap loose but the horse just stood there with his head still turned, eyeballin' me as if to say, "You dumb cluck! Don't you know I'm a kids' horse?" I'd been told, but I didn't believe, so I didn't relax. I moved the horse out, pretty tender for 20 yards or so, and nothing happened, so I touched him with a spur.

That's when he come uncorked. I thought he was really buckin', but after a few jumps I realized he was jumpin' pretty high but he wasn't hittin' the ground too hard. Seemed like every time I got a little loose he'd buck back underneath me again.

I could see that I could ride him and I could also see the oldtimers watchin', so for their sake, I took off my hat and fanned him "oldtimer" style. I seen 'em smile and I sure felt good.

I figured it was gettin' time to get to work, so I pulled up the horse's head. Surprisingly he stopped buckin'.

The boss come up to me and says, "Stu, what did you let him do that for? You should have stopped him earlier."

"I was just tryin' to stay with him, boss," I says.

"He won't do anything like that if you don't spur him," he replied.

I come to find out that the kids on the outfit was my age and had bought the horse a couple of years before for a practice horse. He'd buck when you spurred him but would hardly do anything without bein' spurred. I also found out that the old timers wasn't necessarily grinnin' approval. They was just grinnin' 'cause they'd seen better rides on that horse before.

Twinkle bucked me off later that day. I reached out a little too far to rope a calf, unintentionally touched him with a spur and he went to buckin'. I found myself lying on the ground, unintentionally, with Twinkle lookin' at me with that look in his eye that says, "You dumb cluck. I'm just a kids' horse!"

Runnin' Backwards

I was workin' on an outfit that was located right in the middle of some real good hay growin' country. The outfit I worked for run a couple of hundred cows an' sold surplus hay. There wasn't much ridin' to do on a regular basis durin' the summer, we turned the cows loose on the forest an' they pretty well took care of themselves. The only ridin' we'd do was to spread some salt an' scatter the bulls. The horses was generally in good shape by the time the fall gather come an' for the first couple of weeks durin' the gather they was pretty soft.

Lookin' for some more horse power to help out durin' the fall gather, I agreed to break a neighbor's horse one summer if I could use him in the fall. The arrangement worked out pretty well, I got the horse in the middle of the summer an' figured I had two months to try an' make a horse out of him before he'd start earnin' his keep.

The horse wasn't much to look at an' was one of them kind that would only be loved if he could excel at something. He was a big, rough, roman-nosed horse, a red roan. In a bunch of horses, he wouldn't stand out for any reason. But if a feller looked past the roman-nose an' ignored the roughness, he might could see a horse. Leastways, I thought I could, an' I thought I could see a mighty stout horse.

I saddled him up the afternoon he was brought in. I didn't have any trouble gettin' the saddle on, but then I didn't expect any. I was told he'd been rode before.

But I was surprised when I went to lead him to the center of the corral. Ol' Roany didn't lead too well under a saddle. I checked the cinch an' there was plenty of room there. I couldn't figure out why the horse didn't want to move. All he'd do was back up.

"Just pull him around with the tractor some to get him headed in the right direction. You got to teach him what way to go first!" It was one of the farm hands talkin' an' he was foolin' about the tractor.

I started to move Ol' Roany again, but got the same results as the first time, only a little more determined to go backwards.

"Why don't you get on an' ride him? He don't look like a show horse, so he don't have to know how to lead."

I did get on the horse but he didn't do anything. A touch of the spurs didn't produce anything either. I decided some kind of reaction would be better than none at all, so I tickled Ol' Roany with my spurs an' brought the end of my reins down smartly over his rump.

What I was lookin' for was a response, preferably wanting the horse to move forward. What I got wasn't what I bargained for. Instead of movin' forward, the horse went straight up, as far as he could go. He come down straight legged an' didn't volunteer to do anything else.

I righted myself in the saddle an' spurred him some more. This time he didn't go forward or upward, he went backward. The corral stopped him an' by this time one of the hands had saddled a snubbin' horse an' we proceeded to show Ol' Roany what the forward gear was all about.

I spent a lot of time that summer ridin' Ol' Roany, bein' led by one of the hands. I packed him when we took salt to the forest. The horse didn't know the meaning of the word forward. After a little snubbin', he'd generally loosen up some an' walk out a little freer. He'd generally try to run backwards when I saddled him an' occasionally he'd spook at something an' run backwards. The snubber come in pretty handy, helpin' to keep Ol' Roany's front feet on the ground an' his tail follown' his head rather than his head follown' his tail!

I started ridin' him in the corral without the snubber, an' as he worked out a little better, I'd move him into a larger corral. It wasn't long before I was ridin' Ol' Roany out in the pastures without a snub man. He turned pretty well for a green broke horse an' he stopped good enough so as I wasn't worried about a runaway. Thoughts of him startin' off backward had pretty much left my mind, an' he hadn't offered to buck since I first saddled him. I was sorta lookin' forward to ridin' him on the roundup.

I saddled him up one morning to ride out an' check some stock we kept close to the main ranch. A couple of kids came around the corner on a motorcycle an' Ol' Roany spooked. He bucked a couple of times through the farm machinery an' started runnin' down the lane. I finally got him stopped about a quarter mile away.

Ol' Roany was still a little scared. Too scared to move in fact. He wouldn't turn in any direction an' he wouldn't move forward. I spurred him some an' he still wouldn't move, so I spurred him some more an' he started, but he started backwards an' he started runnin'.

Now this horse could run backwards as fast as most horses could run frontwards. It's sorta hard to get a horse runnin' backwards stopped. The harder I pulled on the reins, the faster Ol' Roany would go an' the more I spurred him, the faster he'd go. The only problem was that he was goin' backwards.

I did get him circlin', but he come to a little rise in the ground an' started over backwards. I decided to quit him before he got too much of a sunburn on his belly.

I pushed myself out of the saddle an' cleared an area for Ol' Roany to land. When he come down, I grabbed a rein so as I wouldn't have to walk back to the ranch.

Ol' Roany got back on his feet, but he was still kinda nervous. He wouldn't hold still, but kept circlin' me while I got on. Leastways, he was headed forward when I hit the saddle. I let him run some then slowed him down. But I didn't stop him. I figured as long as we were movin' forward it was the right direction, an' it didn't matter where we was headed. I didn't much care for the sudden shift into reverse.

Fancy Broomtails

I don't think there's a cowboy alive that doesn't like to run horses. I know I do. On the dude outfits I worked on, I'd generally bring the horses in on a run. I'd do it when I had to take my turn at jinglin' on the cow outfits too. There's just something about a bunch of horses runnin' that does somethin' to a feller. I don't know whether it's the sound, the dust, the sight or the excitement, but somethin' stirs a man's blood.

There's been a time or two when the excitement of runnin' horses has gone a little too far, an' many a dude string has been known to pass up the open gate of a corral an' continue on to unknown adventures. A feller has a lot of work to do when he's runnin' horses, whether they're wild or tame or somewhere in between. He has to be in the right place at the right time.

Runnin' wild horses is against the law now, but a few years ago it wasn't, an' many a cowboy has been known to chase some broomtails if his horse was fresh enough. I've been known to run a few mustangs on occasion durin' work an' after work.

I've also been known to go out an' hunt a few mustangs. By huntin' 'em I mean goin' out with the sole purpose of catching some–maybe a wild colt to break or a stray mare that had got picked up by a mustang bunch.

I was workin' on an outfit one time an' the wild horse population was gettin' a little out of hand. The local ranchers decided to have a mustang hunt as the range was gettin' a little crowded an' there wasn't enough feed for both the cattle an' mustangs.

We decided that the horses caught would be sold at public sale after those with a brand on 'em were cut out an' suckin' colts were "mothered up". Each of the riders would get his choice of one horse out of the mustangs, along with his regular wages, if he helped out. Anybody who roped a mustang an' led him, drove him, or fought him back to camp couldn't have his pick of the horses in the corral 'cause each man was entitled to only one unbranded horse.

What made this hunt interestin' was some real good horses in these broomtails. Earlier there were some remount studs turned loose on the range an' they'd picked up some blooded mares in their bands. Them colts with some 'breedin' an' mustang blood in 'em were highly prized in this rough country. There were a few of these horses on the different outfits in the country an' they were mighty hard to try an' buy.

For this particular horse hunt I picked a little horse called Luigi. He'd been caught out on the desert as a two-year-old, broke an' turned into a pretty good cow horse. He wasn't too fast–a feller had to sneak up on somethin' if he wanted to rope it–but he was tough an' he had the stamina to run mustangs.

He had only one fault. You couldn't get him close enough to a mustang to rope one. He'd just trail along behind, keepin' up but never gettin' close enough to throw a rope. I guess some fellers could have caught mustangs ridin' him if they could throw a rope 40 feet an' still have a loop at the end to catch somethin' with. I couldn't.

Anyway, I didn't figure on catchin' anythin' that day. There were lots of horses an' I thought I could make a better pick when we had the mustangs corraled. Not everybody figured the way I did, an' there were a few fellers who figured on bringin' in their own horses.

One feller, a rancher south of the outfit I worked for, wanted to catch a particular horse. I don't know how true his claims were, but he claimed this particular stud had stolen some of his mares an' he'd been tryin' to catch him for two years without success. The horse was just too smart for him.

This rancher, I'll call him Joe, wanted to do his horse huntin' in the country where this roan stud he'd been chasin' did his ramblin'. Joe, myself, an' another puncher called Ole, had decided to ride the country between the outfit I worked for an' Joe's ranch. This was where the roan stud ran his band.

It was a dry year an' we came upon the stud an' his bunch in a canyon. I thought it strange the stud would allow himself to be in such a situation, but maybe he was lookin' for water. It was a bad place for the stallion because he was cut off on three sides. He did have an exit, but Joe closed it off promptly.

By doin' this, Joe started the mares past Ole an' me. It was all right 'cause we had to start 'em back that way to get 'em into the trap anyway. The stud fell in behind the mares an' Joe was right on his tail, sayin' somethin' 'bout "catchin' that son-of-a-sea-cook now!"

Generally, when we run mustangs, we'd ride with a loose cinch. This gives the horse more room to breathe an' Joe rode the same way. He didn't even stop to tighten his cinch. Joe was closer to catchin' that roan stud than he'd been in two years an' he didn't want to miss an opportunity.

Joe couldn't have been more than six feet behind the stud when he rode past Ole an' me, his rope swingin' an' set to throw. I don't know why, but Joe was tied hard an' fast.

Ole hollered somethin' to him 'bout not havin' his cinch tight an' I yelled 'bout bein' tied hard an' fast but he didn't pay us no mind. He had his prize in sight an' he was goin' to get him one way or the other. Joe's loop snaked out an' it was true. It settled around the stud's neck, a little low, an' Joe put the brakes on his horse. But the stud didn't stop. He kept right on goin', snappin' Joe's latigo an' pullin' Joe's saddle right over his horse's neck, with Joe still in it.

When the saddle was in midair, half way between the roan stud an' Joe's bewildered horse, Joe left the saddle. He hit the ground pretty hard but was up mighty quick, caught his horse, jumped on him bareback an' started out after the stud an' his saddle. Ole stopped him by mentionin' that the mares were gettin' away.

I started out to haze the mares an' it wasn't long before Joe an' Ole showed up to help. We got the mares headed into the trap, got 'em locked in an' went to see if we could retrieve Joe's saddle.

The stud left a mighty plain trail with that saddle bouncin' along behind him. It wasn't long before we started to find pieces of Joe's saddle scattered in the sagebrush. First we found his slicker, then a stirrup, then a little farther on, part of his cinch.

It was gettin' late an' Joe figured he'd better get back to his ranch, get a fresh horse an' another saddle, an' continue the hunt in the mornin'. Ole suggested he bring along a pack horse to carry back the different parts of his saddle as he found 'em.

We rode back to the horse trap an' checked to see that the mustangs were still there an' that they had feed an' water. Then we left.

Next mornin' Joe started out after the roan stud. He got what was left of his saddle when it lodged between some rocks. Joe said he ended up cuttin' the rope with his pocket knife, leavin' part of it draggin' on the stud. He said he figured he wouldn't have anythin' to do in his spare time if he couldn't chase that stud, an' the frayed end of the lariat rope would make it easy for him to catch his trail in the future.

Joe ended up pickin' out a roan colt that looked just like his daddy for his choice in the wild horse hunt. He was heard a few years later to remark that the roan horse was one of the best he'd ever ridden. Maybe that's one reason most of the horses on Joe's outfit now are roans an' why he'd always had roans an' why he'd let the roan stud free when he had him.

A Familiar Habit

I buckarooed out in Nevada for some time on quite a few different cattle outfits, some good, some not so good. I enjoyed the work and liked seein' new an' different country. Nevada is the only area of the country where methods used in the cattle business a hundred years ago are still generally accepted.

One of the outfits I worked for was in eastern Nevada. It was a good outfit. The horses were good for the most part, an' the food was the best I'd ever had on a cow outfit. This ranch also had a mighty nice reputation among the other cow outfits an' all the cowboys around.

So I was mighty surprised to hear that when a neighbor's stud got loose an' was runnin' with our mares, we were goin' to send a couple of boys to castrate him. A good stallion was mighty valuable in this country an' it seemed to go against the grain to cut someone's stud, without tryin' to return the horse or at least hold him until the rightful owners were notified.

I was mighty apprehensive when I was told to ride my stoutest rope horse the next mornin'. Everybody knew what was goin' on, but it didn't seem right. I can sure appreciate the need to keep stock separated, but I figured these were some mighty drastic measures.

The cowboss was scatterin' riders, tellin' some where to drop off salt an' others where to move how many cattle where. I didn't get any orders until everybody had moved out, some of 'em trailin' three or four pack horses loaded with salt.

"Stu, you an' Pat follow me. We got a little job to do, then we'll move some cows around an' then bring a sick cow home."

I noticed as the cowboss told us what to do that Pat was mounted on a stout horse an' the cowboss, while he always rode good horses, had a good stout horse today.

This was the day the stud would be altered an' the cowboss, Pat an' myself were goin' to do it. I had some questions as to the legality of what we were doin', so I asked the cowboss.

"Don't worry about it, Stu," he replied.

But I did worry about it. I could see myself sittin' in the sheriff's office, answerin' questions an' bein' led to a cell in the county jail house.

We located the stud an' mares an' didn't have a hard time workin' them into a pen some miles away. As I recall, after we'd separated the stud from the mares an' turned the mares loose, the cowboss caught the horse's head. Pat caught the front legs an' I missed the heels. Another throw didn't catch anything. The next throw I caught the heels an' the stud went down. Don't think I was missin' those throws on purpose. I was doin' the best I could even though I imagined the sheriff was hidin' behind every sagebrush. I thought I faced a certain jail sentence if I got caught.

The cowboss did a good job of castratin' the stallion after he went down. He was mighty careful tying the cords with hair pulled from the horse's tail. We didn't want the horse to bleed to death; we just wanted to curtail his activities.

The operation was completed an' we were about to turn the horse loose when Pat says, "Let's mark this horse. Bob his tail or somethin' so everyone who sees him knows who did the job."

"Good idea, Pat," says the cowboss. "What should we do, make him look like a mule?"

"Yep. Bell his tail an' roach his mane."

I didn't say a word. I sure didn't want to draw attention to a horse I'd helped castrate illegally, but I was overruled.

When the horse got up, he had three bells in his tail an' a roached mane, which is almost a crime in Nevada on a good cow outfit. He looked like a mule.

We left an' finished the rest of the day's ridin'. I was still apprehensive. I was part of a criminal act an' if I wasn't a criminal, at least I was a criminal's helper. I could see myself standin' in front of a judge sayin' I was only doin' what I was told.

I was mighty silent about the incident an' almost had heart failure when the older hands, who had heard what we'd done, was braggin' an' laughin' about it in town. When asked if I was involved, I generally left without answerin' to keep from incriminating myself.

I found out a few months later that I hadn't really helped commit a crime. The owner of the horse was a small horse rancher who couldn't afford to hire help on his place. The cowboss said it was a "familiar habit" to find his young stallions with someone else's mares. The offended rancher would generally send his hands out to cut the stallions for the owner. Accordin' to the cowboss, the reason we marked the stud was to inform the owner the job was done. Each ranch had its own method of markin' the horse so the owner would know who to thank next time he was in the area.

I'd spent a lot of time worryin' about what would happen to me if we got caught in the act, only to find out we were doin' a favor for the owner of the horse.

Goin' Home

A loose cinch has caused plenty of cowboys a lot of problems. Most of the time, a feller will ride with a cinch just tight enough to keep the saddle in place under normal conditions. Where the problems occur is when a feller has some heavy work to do an' he don't take the time to take the slack out an' tighten his cinch.

Openin' a gate ain't heavy work, but a cinch tight enough to keep a saddle in place is mighty important. I had a colt one time that I thought might make a pretty good horse if I could ever break him. I called him Nick an' he was hard to ride an' hard to catch. Most generally, if a feller could ride Nick the first 20 minutes, he had him rode for the day.

I'd been ridin' Nick for a couple of months an' he was startin' to come around. I tried to ride him every day, generally in the afternoon when we rode smaller circles an' the work wouldn't be too much for him. We was workin' cattle most of the time an' the boss on this outfit was more interested in gettin' the cattle work done than in makin' good horses. So I didn't necessarily have the time to correct or rework his mistakes.

But I did start workin' him on gates. Sometimes he didn't get quite close enough an' I'd have to do some stretchin' to reach the latch, but it was gettin' the work done rather than makin' a good horse.

One day I had a gate to open an' didn't have much time to do it. Granted, I could have opened it faster on foot, but I liked to take every opportunity I could to give Nick some trainin'. The only problem I had was gettin' Nick as close as I wanted, to open that gate. The fellers was drivin' them cattle to me pretty fast an' I had to get that gate open an' get a count on the cattle when they went through. Nick just wasn't cooperatin' an' my cinch wasn't quite tight enough.

The more I reached for the gate, the more my saddle slid off to the right. I guess this created a peculiar situation for Nick as he was just gettin' used to packin' a saddle on the middle of his back an' this one was slidin' off to one side. The more it slid, the more Nick moved away from it an' the farther I had to stretch for the latch.

I could see Nick eyeballin' me an' it wasn't long before I started wonderin' if I was goin' to get this gate opened. The farther I stretched for the latch, the farther Nick moved away from it. I found myself out on a limb so to speak, but there wasn't no limb.

At this point I had three choices. First choice, I could continue spurrin' my saddle skirts tryin' to get Nick to move into me an' closer to the gate. I was doin' this but wasn't gettin' any results.

Second, I could lunge for the gate hopin' to grab onto it an' keep Nick at the same time.

Third, I could try to get off gracefully. The second an' third choices seemed most promisin', as I was gettin' tired of leanin' on thin air an' tryin' to reach the latch.

I was ponderin' the three plans an' tryin' to decide which one would be best when Nick made up my mind for me. I guess he got tired of foolin' around, cause he left me in mid air. It was a choice I hadn't figured on an' not even close to them I was considerin'.

I had a split second in mid air before I hit the ground. When I picked myself up I decided that none of my three choices was very good. I opened the gate an' counted the cattle as they went in. Nick had long since left for home; the last I saw of him was his tail, an' my saddle under his belly.

Paul, the foreman, rode up to me an' asked, "Where's your horse, Stu? You an' Nick have an argument?" "Paul," I says, "Nick an' me didn't have an argument. It was a matter of choices."

"Choices?"

"Yep."

"What was the choices?"

"Well," I says, "I had one choice of three to make, an' Nick only had one choice of two to make."

"What was your choices?"

"Don't concern yourself with my choices, Paul. The fact of the matter is that Nick had fewer choices to make than I did an' it was easier for him to make up his mind. His choices wasn't near as complicated as the choices I had to make."

"What was his choices?"

"His choices was pretty easy. He just had to make up his mind as to whether he wanted to go home or stay 'til the job was done. He decided to go home. I really wasn't in a position to change his mind. Uh, how 'bout a lift?"

Chocolate Chip

Runnin a dude ranch can be a pretty good job, as long as the ranch is set up to handle the guests. But when the ranch doesn't have the facilities to handle dudes, guests or freeloaders can be a problem and a nuisance.

I worked on a ranch that solved the problem of uninvited guests pretty quick an' real slick. The outfit wasn't set up to handle dudes, there weren't any sleeping quarters for extra people or an extra cook to help out with those chores. Sleeping quarters was kinda crowded in the main house an' the teenage boys was shuffled off to the bunkhouse with the hired hands. This didn't work out too well; the city slickers was used to stayin' up late an' gettin' up late. Of course, with the hands it was just the opposite. As it turned out, there was usually some friction in the bunkhouse when the uninvited guests arrived.

The cook had the roughest time. She was actually the boss' wife. She did a mighty good job of cookin' for the family an' the hands, but she kept herself wore to a frazzle cookin' for the extra people. As this was the summer ranch, the cookin' was a bit harder as she didn't have an electric stove. The hands was always mighty helpful, keepin' the woodbox full an' takin' turns with the dishes. But nobody looked forward to the extra chores the freeloaders caused. For instance, the hands always took their dishes to the sink, whereas the "guests" generally left their dishes, an' the hands found themselves as poorly dressed busboys.

These strangers also needed help gettin' horses saddled an' bridled. When they brought the horses back, they was generally well used an' in worse shape than they'd been in since the last freeloaders used 'em. An' all the hollerin' an' screamin' of the kids runnin' around an' gettin' underfoot kept the ranch in a general uproar. Yet the boss an' his wife were easy goin' an' I don't know of them ever turnin' down one of the freeloaders, although some subtle hints was carefully ignored by the uninvited guests.

After one particularly tryin' weekend, the boss' wife was standin' by the gate watchin' one carload of freeloaders drive away as what appeared to be another load was pullin' in. I was changin' horses when the boss lady calls me over.

"Stu, could you do me a favor before supper tonight?"

"Sure," I says.

I was real surprised at her request a few hours later. "Run over to the neighbors and borrow a sack of sheep manure. You might want to take a shovel along and I'll get you a sack. I'll want it fairly clean."

Later that afternoon, I found myself in the neighbor's corral, 20 miles from home, shovelin' sheep manure into a brown paper sack. I was kinda surprised at the size of the sack she'd given me; she couldn't hardly fertilize the flower bed with that sack of manure, so I filled it as full as I could get it an' borrowed another sack an' filled it so as there would be plenty.

Your fertilizer is out in the woodshed, I says when I got back.

"Well, bring it in the house!"

"Both them sacks I filled for you?"

"Both sacks? I only gave you one."

"Well, the sack you gave me wasn't hardly big enough to get enough manure in it to fertilize anything, so I got a gunny sack full plus the small sack you gave me."

"Oh, I see," she said. "Well, bring it in."

"In the kitchen?"

"No. Just bring it up to the house, and just bring the sack I gave you. I don't need the gunny sack right now."

"Here's your fertilizer," I says as I handed her the sack.

"Oh, that's not fertilizer," she replied as she looked into the sack. "This is much too dirty. Would you mind cleaning it up for me?"

"No," I says. "But how?"

"Just shake it on a screen. What I need is pure manure! I don't need any corral dust mixed in."

So I found myself cleanin' sheep manure, usin' an old window screen. When I was done, I had the cleanest manure on the ranch an' probably in the state. The boss lady wouldn't tell me what she wanted it for or why it had to be so clean, an' I was glad to give it to her when it was clean enough.

I'd forgot about it until the next day when I went to sneak a fresh cookie the boss lady had just baked an' got caught. Normally, a feller could get any kind of a snack at any time without gettin' cussed, but on this day, I got into hot water about it an' I'd been caught red-handed. I started to leave, but the boss lady called me back.

"Stu," she says, "the fertilizer you got for me yesterday is in those cookies."

"Huh?! "

"Last night I melted down all the chocolate we had, poured it over these "lamb pellets" and set them out to dry. This morning, after the chocolate had set up, I mixed them in with the cookie dough and you just about ate the finished product. These will be for our guests only after supper."

"I'm sure glad you warned me. I don't think I want any of them cookies."

"I'll make sure," she continued, "that none of the hands get any of these, but don't you tell anybody. I'm going to put an end to all this free-loading once and for all. These people that came yesterday will let everybody in town know what happened and it will ruin my reputation as a cook, but we've got to stop this freeloading. People eating us out of house and home, riding our horses into the ground, this just can't go on! Just inviting themselves in. Someday we might be able to invite the people we want up here."

I didn't wait for her to finish as she seemed to be gettin' a load off her mind.

And I couldn't wait around after supper to see how the cookies went over, I had to reset a shoe on a horse. But the hands told me the cookies didn't go over too well. Seems like nobody could get more than one cookie down then they went to bed! Early.

The next mornin' they were up an' on their way, early. They suddenly remembered that they had to be someplace else on that particular day an' left, even before breakfast. No amount of coaxin' could convince them to stay, even for breakfast.

As the summer progressed, the uninvited guests dropped in less frequently and everybody could get their jobs done without extra help from the arm chair experts. And the boss lady was even seen more often doin' a little more ridin' than she had done the past few years, an' she seemed to be enjoyin' the ranch more. She had effectively solved the problem of uninvited guests, although she had to make certain promises to get the invited guests to come out.

Drifter

Drifter was a good lookin' sorrel horse that come to the dude outfit early in June. From his looks, I figured him to be 'bout half Arab and half Quarter. Walt was to try him first an' most of the fellers figured Walt was pretty lucky, till he almost got his teeth knocked out tryin' to catch him. The fellers soon learned that Drifter shouldn't be caught from the rear. The story that come with the horse was that his previous owners had mistreated him an' he had just enough fightin' blood in him that he needed some special care an' treatment durin' his trainin' lessons. He'd been rode some but was considered treacherous and undependable by his previous owners. He'd had plenty of horse trainers take a try at him, but for one reason or another he was still labeled bad. All he had to do on this outfit was pack a dude around for a few hours a day an' he'd have a pretty secure future.

After a few years he "might make a passable dude horse, but right now he's too much horse for most dudes" was the general opinion of the horse. Consequently, he wasn't rode much an' the boss was figurin' on sendin' him to the sale. Those times he was rode, he was rode by one of the hands an' they'd generally cuss him up one side an' down the other when they got back. I'd got to thinkin' that I wouldn't mind ridin' a good lookin' horse like Drifter if I could find some way to ride him an' watch the dudes, too.

I'd been ridin' a buckskin horse with a big white spot on her hip, an' I figured the boss would soon want to start dudin' her. If I was goin' to have to take another horse, I'd just as soon be able to pick him as to have the boss give him to me. So one morning, I throws my rig on Drifter an' says, "I'd sorta like to try this horse for a few days."

I went to ridin' Drifter every day. I had to experiment with a few different bits before I found something that seemed to work pretty good. But I still wasn't a hundred percent satisfied. On a hunch one mornin' I thought I'd try a hackamore. The horse always seemed to be fightin' the bit, so l figured I'd take it away from him.

The hackamore seemed to do the trick. With one less thing to worry about, Drifter has a little more time to concentrate on what we was doin' an' I was beginnin' to look forward to ridin' him after a couple of days. He was still a little nervous 'bout his hind feet, but it was kinda nice to be ridin' a horse that nobody else wanted. His habit with his hind feet worked out pretty well; I didn't have to lead too many kids around for a couple of hours, which really got to be a drag.

Drifter was a pretty good horse, but his main fault was that he had too much energy. He was the kind of horse that needed to be rode on a regular basis or he'd be hard to handle the next day. An' a horse that's hard to handle on a dude outfit ain't worth much. There's too many problems with

the dudes to be worried about the horses. I noticed Drifter seemed to like bein' rode the more he was rode. An' the more he was rode, the better he got. Bein' a good horse to start with would have been in his favor, but he was gettin' better. The fact that he was a good lookin' horse didn't help much, 'cause every time I'd get him rode down to where he was half decent, the boss would want to use him.

Usually, when the boss used a horse on that outfit, he rode it for an hour an' then let the horse stand in the corral the rest of the day. This wasn't the type of work Drifter needed. After a couple of days of this, Drifter would start feelin' himself an' the boss would have his saddle put on another horse.

When it come time to shoe Drifter, the experience with Walt stood out in everybody's mind. I was lookin' to get a little help puttin' shoes on the horse, but nobody was willin' an' I don't like to shoe horses anyway. I was kinda reluctant to do it 'cause I didn't want to shoe my horse for the boss. 'Course there was other horses, but I'd made the mistake of marryin' myself to the horse, an' a feller shouldn't do it in a business where he's ridin' horses for somebody else.

I worked it out with the boss where if I shod Drifter, I wouldn't have to lend him the horse, 'cept when there was photographers doin' publicity kind of stuff. Well, the horse did look good wearin' my rig. Long as I could use the horse when I wanted it was OK with me. As it come about, I used Drifter every day I wanted for the rest of the season. He turned out to be one of the best horses on the place for the hands, but he was never duded. He was all horse, an' one that I figure got the insight to. That hackamore was what done the trick.

A Real Cowboy

When I was goin' to college, I took a couple of colts to break so I could earn some extra money an' help out with the expenses. I was gettin' a dollar a day to ride these colts an' I figured it was worth it just to be able to get away from the books for a while an' get paid for it. As it worked out, I couldn't give the horses all the ridin' they needed or all I wanted, but we kept at it on a fairly regular basis.

One of these colts was givin' me some problems. He was a brown horse, sorta plain with no outstandin' features. His owner wanted him for a kid horse, but I was havin' some doubts about how well he'd turn out. What ridin' I'd given him wasn't workin' the hump out of his back. He'd never really offered to buck, but every time I rode him I felt like I was sittin' on a time bomb with a short fuse.

I'd got to ridin' the other colts with my neighbor in the foothills occasionally, an' I figured it was 'bout time to take old Brownie out an' put some really wet saddle blankets on him. It was 'bout time this brown horse started doin' somethin' besides standin' in a corral.

Things went pretty well for a while. We had some fields to ride through before we got to the foothills, an' this was a good place to move the horses out some an' get 'em to loosen up. Even though I loped the brown horse in figure eights an' circles, I still felt like he wasn't loose.

There was some irrigation pipe we had to cross before we left the field. We started around it, but I says to myself, "Ho! I'm breakin' this horse, an' I guess I should teach this bronc to go over this kinda stuff."

So I turns the horse around an' starts him over the pipe. His front half goes over okay, but he drags a hind foot over the pipe, it rolls over an' the sprinkler head crashes down into some bushes.

Now I'm not sure what happened next. The brown horse started buckin', an I'm purty certain I rode him two jumps 'cause I felt three real hard thuds an' the next thing I knew I was layin' on the ground with one rein in my hand. I figure I rode him two jumps an' the third thud I felt was me hittin' the ground. 'Course, I might have only rode him one jump, hit the ground an' bounced, but I'm stickin' to the idea I rode him two jumps.

I still had one rein, even though the horse was draggin' me along the ground. I finally lost control of him when I let the rein slip from my hand. I really didn't lose control – I'd lost that already – but I did lose my horse.

Layin there on the ground, I was sorta glad I wasn't tryin' to sit in that saddle the way the brown horse was buckin' an' the way them stirrups was poppin' over the empty seat. My neighbor caught the horse an' I checked myself over. No broken bones, but I had a cut over one eye that was bleedin' some.

"This horse has drawed first blood," I thought. I figured I'd show him a thing or two as my neighbor led him up to me.

"You okay?" he asked. "What happened?"

"Just a little misunderstanding between this critter an' me," I said as I climbed back in the saddle. "We're goin' to get this straightened out right now."

I set down in the saddle an' give the brown horse a feel of my quirt an' spurs. I couldn't get more than a crowhop or two from him an' when he stopped, the hump in his back was gone. He seemed to be a different horse.

We continued to ride to the foothills an' that day I put a lot of miles on 'ole Brownie an' they was kinda hard miles. It didn't hurt him none an' after the buckin' episode, both the horse an' me relaxed some.

Brownie was gettin' tired when we got to the neighbors an' I could see my wife doin' some yard work. I figured I looked a sight, ridin' up to the house with dried blood over one side of my face.

"Bucked you off, huh!"

"Well, me an' the horse did have an argument which I temporarily lost," I replied.

"You better turn him loose and let me doctor that cut," she said.

I turned the horse loose an' let her put some medicine over my eye. It wasn't 'til a couple of days later that my wife told me my neighbor thought I was a real cowboy.

"How come?" I asked.

"He says you're a real cowboy because you didn't let go of the reins when that horse bucked you off!"

"I wouldn't believe that," I says. "I just don't know when I'm bucked off!"

The Talker

One of the necessary jobs on a cow outfit is shoein' horses. All cowboys are expected to do it, but I never met any that really liked it. I know I sure don't like it an' I generally feel a lot better when my horses was shod an' I didn't have to worry about it for a few weeks.

On one outfit I rode for, out in Nevada, there wasn't any set time to shoe horses. Occasionally, in the afternoon, the cowboss would have the remuda run in an' the buckaroos would have to shoe the pack horses an' a few work horses that was bein' used. A feller was expected to keep the horses in his string shod on his own time.

I never much cared for the group sessions of horse shoein' on this outfit. The work horses would generally lean on a feller pretty heavy an' the pack horses, well, the pack horses was a different matter.

We had two rough string riders on the outfit an' they had their hands pretty well full with their own strings. If another feller had wanted to ride the rough string, he'd have been given his pick of any of the pack horses. The cowboss hoped all the pack horses would eventually end up in the cowboy's strings, but he also realized that all cowboys weren't buckin' horse riders.

Bein' hard to shoe wasn't a qualification for a horse to end up in the rough string or packin' string. These horses was tough an' unpredictable. They could be counted on to buck every time somebody strapped a saddle on 'em. They could also be counted on to bite, strike or kick any unsuspectin' hand that happened to be close enough to offer a target. Most of them horses needed more handlin' an' ridin' than they got.

That's one of the reasons I didn't like the group shoein' sessions. Sometimes it got downright dangerous.

Another reason I didn't care for these sessions was tempers. With seven or eight of these educated broncs tied up to a fence an' the same number of buckaroos tryin' to dress 'em up with a new set of shoes, a wrong move by one man or horse could, an' generally would, have disastrous results.

I'm all for discipline of horses. A lot of times a good slap on the rump with a rasp is all that's needed to get a little cooperation from the horse.

Shoein' horses is hard work an' many cowboys tend to give out major punishment for minor offenses when shoein'. On this outfit, when somebody doled out some punishment durin' the group shoein' session, rightly or wrongly, it set off a chain reaction.

Horses started buckin' while tied to the fence, halters an' lead ropes snapped, cowboys was bein' bowled over an' scramblin' out of the way, equipment was bein' knocked over an' a loose horse or two added to the general confusion. No, I didn't much care to join these group sessions. Some of the horses in my string were a little touchy 'bout a feller messin' with their feet.

I had a horse in my string that had had his beginnin's in the pack string. He had some years on him by the time I got him, an' I'm sure glad somebody took the time to make a fairly gentle horse out of him.

As I recall, he was called Pat, an' I only used him when I had short circles to ride or if it was my turn to try an' rope some calves durin' the brandin'.

One afternoon when the cowboss had the remuda run in so as the buckaroos could shoe some of the pack horses, I caught up Pat, figurin' on puttin' on a new set of walkin' instruments after supper. I'm mighty glad that I did 'cause the afternoon's activity resulted in part of the corral fence bein' torn down. While I was shoein' Pat, the other buckaroos was repairin' the corral under the direction of the cowboss.

This was the first time I'd shod ol' Pat, still bein' new to the outfit, an' I'd heard he wasn't easy to shoe an' mighty touchy, even downright serious 'bout his feet. But I started in, talkin' to myself for courage more than any other reason. I picked up all his feet an' stuck shoes on 'em without too much trouble. He did try to take a foot an' place it on me occasionally, but we talked ourselves out of that an' anything that might result.

Only later did I find out that Pat always had to be throwed to be shod. I used the horse for a long time on that outfit, sparingly, an' never had to throw him to shoe him. But every time I had to shoe him or any other horse in my string, I done it after supper an' always talked to the horse. An' I made sure nobody was around.

Shoein' horses my way does have some advantages. I usually didn't have too much trouble with the horse, didn't have to put up with well intentioned but poor advice, an' I never lost an' argument!

Saddle Sores...
...can leave you holding the horse

A few years ago I was running a dude ranch up in the Grand Teton country of Wyoming. It was a pretty little ranch with some real good horses, nice country and nice people. It had the makings for a nice year.

Generally, when a dude wrangler has a few spare moments, he's surrounded by his visitors with questions pertaining to horses and riding. This was no exception. On this particular occasion, a woman slightly overweight explained that she was having problems staying with her horse at the trot. Her horse seemed to be coming up when she was going down. To make matters worse, the reverse always happened when she was going up. This situation was causing her some discomfort, particularly on the insides of her legs, which were, according to her, rubbed absolutely raw. She wanted to continue riding during her vacation, but the pain she was suffering was unbearable.

As I listened, I sized her up. Just as nice a person as you ever want to meet, pleasant and always smiling, yet she had the uncanny ability to do just about everything wrong. She was continually creating small disasters everywhere she went. These situations never hurt anyone, seriously, but they made her ripe for jokes, puns and continual ribbing. Fortunately for her, she was good-natured and she took her small misfortunes in stride. This was the first time I had seen her in a dejected mood.

I decided I was gonna try and help her with her problem. "Well," I said, "it takes a lot of experience or a lot of years ridin' to be able to ride without gettin' sore, but I think we might be able to help you some."

Her face lit up some as I proceeded to give her riding hints, but I figured it would take her a long time to really get the feel of a horse. The next morning I helped her some more by giving her a different horse to ride. 'Ol Blue, the horse she had been riding, was rough in all forms of travel. Her replacement this morning was smoother gaited, which should help my visitor's problem some.

I was kinda surprised to see her down at the corrals that afternoon seeking a little more advice on how to solve her problem. We reviewed the riding tips I'd given her the day before; I explained why I'd switched horses for her. Hopefully I reassured her that it would take some time and practice before she could ride without chaffing her legs.

She had been working at the tips I had given her and she knew that it would take some time and practice. "But," she pondered, "what would you think of my insulatin' my legs against getting rubbed until I learn how to ride?"

"Where in the world did you get that idea?" I asked.

"My husband suggested it last night. Would it work?" She sounded like she was really hoping, almost praying.

"Well," I said, "I dunno. What would you use?"

"My husband suggested foam rubber and the ranch is sending a truck into town for groceries. I could place an order for some!" Her voice was starting to get excited, like she was anticipating a sore-free vacation.

"I don't think that foam rubber would be too practical," I stated. "You might do better to wear two pair of pants or even to buy some 'long handles'. As a matter of fact, there's some cowboys wear 'em year 'round. You might even get 'em real cheap as there ain't much demand for 'em right now, bein' as its summer an' the temperature is real close to ninety some odd degrees."

This idea seemed to go over pretty good. The following day a package from town was delivered to the lady and she went riding that afternoon. I had not noticed it before, but that was the first time she'd gone riding in the afternoon since she'd come to the ranch.

As the afternoon progressed, I took more notice of the lady. She was riding along, talking to everybody, smiling. She looked like she was enjoying herself even though sweat was flooding off her face like she was in the middle of a cloudburst. The temperature was mighty close to 95 degrees that afternoon, but she did remark later that her legs weren't being rubbed quite so bad.

Well, she rode every day until her vacation was over, using her "insulation". She even became better at matching her horse with his up and down movements.

Making A Name For Himself

It was time to move camp. We figured it was time because we were having to ride about 15 to 20 miles from camp every day to make a gather. We were capitalizing on some good weather and camped about 30 miles from the home ranch, getting a good start on the spring branding. Nearly every calf in the country had been branded during the last two weeks, including some of the neighbors'. That was all right though because the neighbors had sent their reps and they made sure their bosses' calves all got the right brand. Still, we were having to ride too far to make a gather worthwhile.

So, Willie and me was selected to help the cook move camp while the other buckaroos made a final gather in the area. They would meet us at the new campsite. Moving camp consisted of taking tents down, throwing them along with bedrolls in the truck, gathering up the cook—his equipment and groceries—and moving up the country some 30-odd miles. Then we had to set it all up again.

It wasn't hard and enough time was spent around the coffee pot between setting up tents and unloading the truck that the cook was getting a little peeved at having us in the way. So Willie set out to do some fishing and I set out to do some exploring around an old mining camp up the canyon a ways.

What I found in that old mining camp sent me running back to camp. One of the items was an old table that was still usable, just what we needed for our card games at night. The other item was an old outhouse that was also still serviceable. Now this camp didn't have all the comforts of home, but I figured it sure would come close with the addition of these two items.

It took longer to drag Willie from his fishing than it did to load this treasure into the truck, place the outhouse near camp and level up the table. The new fixtures met with the approval of all the hands and it wasn't long before we decided to brand on the table the names of everybody who was in camp. But we decided to add an extra feature. We made two columns: one for them that got bucked off and one for them that didn't.

Frank was the first to get his name burned into the table—in the "bucked-off" column. His time came while we were heeling calves up to the branding fire. Somehow or another, Frank's horse got his leg over the rope, and when he jerked up the slack, his horse "come uncorked". Frank only lasted a couple of jumps and I figured he had hurt himself when he lit, but he was OK.

Steve got his from a colt he was riding. I don't know what caused the horse to start bucking, but when he did he really worked at it. Steve was throwed into a fence and the colt pret-near fell on him. There was no harm done to Steve, and they were going to tear out the fence anyway.

Willie got his out of his own carelessness. He had been doctoring a cow for footrot. He finished with the cow, tightened up his cinch and went to get on his horse without untracking him. He was throwed before he hit the saddle. His name went into the "bucked-off" column.

So it went. Eventually all the buckaroos, except the cowboss and me, had their names entered in the "throwed" column, through one happening or another. And a day or two before we were ready to move back to the home ranch, it looked like the cowboss' name and mine wouldn't be entered in the "throwed" column. My name should have been entered though, because I was bucked off the jungle horse, but the hands figured it didn't count since I was bareback.

But I had my name branded someplace else, and I would sure rather have had it in the "throwed" column than where it was.

It happened one morning when I had occasion to use the new outhouse. I had already caught and saddled my horse and was at a loss about what to do with him, because I had loaned my hobbles to somebody else. It occurred to me that I could take the reins, enter the little house and close the door, then knot the reins from the inside. By doing it this way, I could take care of my business and hold my horse at the same time.

This idea worked pretty well until something spooked my horse. He jerked back and pulled the outhouse over, with me still in it. The door was facing the ground. And there I was, trapped inside the outhouse holding the broken end of my reins.

It seemed like a long time before I heard the other hands calling for me. I answered and heard hoofbeats, then the cowboss calling, "Stu, where are you?"

"In here," I answered, somewhat meekly.

"What are you doin' in there?"

"Get me out an' I'll tell you!" I heard a couple of ropes settle on the little house, a couple of grunts and groans by horses and men, and it wasn't long before the little building was righted. I've got to admit though, they sure weren't the gentlest construction crew in the country.

I walked out of the little house kinda sheepishly, holding the broken ends of my reins in one hand. Someone had caught up my horse and as I repaired my reins, somebody remarked how strange it was that I had got bucked off my horse, then hid in the outhouse to keep from getting my name entered on the table in the "throwed" column.

Gettin' a little peeved, I explained how I came to be in the situation I'd just been rescued from. I proved my story by holding up the busted reins.

"Why didn't you just come out and get back on your horse?"

"Partner," I said, "in the predicament I was in, there was only one way out, and I'll be damned if I was going to take it."

We got our job done that day and I was sorta relieved that my name wasn't going to be entered in the "throwed" column. But I was real dismayed when we rode back to camp that afternoon. There it was, staring me in the face. The cook had branded my name. It was bigger than anybody else's. And it was on the outhouse door!

Range Hoss Manners
This horse got his lesson
in wild horse behavior

Horses have always been a big part of ranch life in northern Nevada and southern Idaho. Most of the ranches keep broodmare bands just to fill their remudas. One such outfit I worked for maintained 80 broodmares in different bands.

These stud bunches had free run of the desert and were corralled only once or twice a year. The weaner colts were halter broke and gentled. The other outfits kept the horse colts for replacements, and the fillies they wanted for broodmares. The remainder of the colt crop was sold.

Halter breaking the colts and teaching them some manners gave us something to do besides feed cows during the winter and it paid off. Halter broke colts usually could command a higher price.

The owner of this ranch decided to experiment. He purchased an Appaloosa stallion about four years old. This horse was well mannered and seemed to have the right kind of disposition in addition to having the right kind of build. The owner rode him for a few weeks as his personal saddle horse, then selected 10 or 12 mares and turned this new broodmare band out in a fenced section. This was the only bunch of horses on the place that was fenced in other than the remuda. The owner thought this wise as the young stallion might decide to leave for more familiar surroundings and take some of the mares with him.

He later remarked that in a dream one night, he rode upon this band of horses and each one of the mares had a colt by her side and each colt had the blanket and spotted rump characteristic of the Appaloosa. As he rode towards this band of horses he saw that the colts didn't really have spots on their rumps. Closer inspection revealed that the spots were actually dollar signs! He also said that was one of the most contented nights' sleep he'd ever had.

It wasn't long before we started to have problems with this young stallion and his little harem. He became possessive of his mares. When we had to ride through his pasture, he'd drive his mares off a ways, then come to meet us with his ears back and his teeth bared.

The Appaloosa had been barn raised and had lost all fear of man. The other ranch stallions had enough fear of man in them that they would drive their mares off a good distance and try to stay out of sight when riders approached.

The owner decided something had to be done before his Appaloosa hurt someone. He realized the horse was only following his instincts but the loss of the fear of man complicated the problem somewhat. All the hands had suggestions as to what to do and some of them tried their own suggestions without any noticeable results. I never thought much about the situation, even when Joe dug out a bull whip and started practicing with it.

I'd never had much use for a bull whip. I had plenty of trouble with a regular catch rope, but Joe could use a whip. I'd seen him crack a whip in front of a horse and turn that beast before he could reach a hole in the fence or an open gate.

Joe practiced with that whip for a few days. He even saddled a horse and practiced horseback. I figured he was just killing time. Then the owner says to me one morning, "Stu, catch up your fastest horse. I've got a special job for you and Joe."

I was honored to do this special chore. As I saddled my horse, I was thinking that this special chore might lead to a raise or promotion. I didn't have any idea what we were going to do and I didn't care. I was going to be well mounted. I could handle anything that came my way.

When I asked Joe what we were going to do, he mumbled something about a little fishing and running some horses. I didn't care for the fishing, but I was sure ready to run horses. Every now and then we'd have to run off a bunch of Mustangs that might get too close to the broodmare bunches. The idea was to avert a stud fight and keep our mares from running off with a stranger.

As we rode through the pasture where the Appaloosa and his band were, I was thinking that maybe I could catch me one of those rangs. I was figuring what to do with the rang I was going to catch when the young stallion came out to meet us. I thought we'd let the ill-mannered horse run us around some just like he always did.

As the Appaloosa came closer, Joe held back. He'd brought his whip along and right now it was dragging the ground, a new popper on the end. When the Appaloosa was close enough, Joe hollered, "Stu, lead him to the north! Stay on level ground if you can and don't let him get the inside circle on you!"

I took off. The stallion followed. Joe followed the stallion, whip in hand. We were covering rough ground at a fast pace with the stallion trying to get me and my horse and Joe trying to get the stallion a good lick with the whip.

I recalled that Joe had mentioned fishing, but I didn't realize until now that I was the bait! If I'd known what was on Joe's mind when he was practicing with the whip, I'd have gotten out there and given him some help.

That Appaloosa was doing his best to take chunks out of my horse's rump, and when he'd get close enough to take a chunk out of my leg, I'd slap him across the nose with the ends of my reins.

I was slapping the horse across the nose to slow him down and Joe was using the whip to keep him going.

It wasn't long before the Appaloosa either tired of this treatment or he figured he'd driven me far enough away from his mares. He quit the chase

and turned in the direction of his herd. Joe followed him a hundred yards or so, still using the whip.

I'd found a tree that offered a good amount of shade and loosened the cinches on my saddle when Joe came riding up. We admired how fast our horses were.

"That's the button-hole treatment," said Joe, "and now that we've started it, we'll have to keep it up every day 'til that young smart alec learns to start acting like a regular range stud."

"Button-hole treatment?"

"Yep. Every time I could, I'd try to cut a button hole out of that horse's hide. Just a small one, of course. He'll learn faster and we can quit when he starts to drive his mares away and stay away from any riders when they approach."

"That sounds OK to me," I replied, "but how come you picked me to be your bait?"

"Well, you're a long ways from being the heaviest puncher on this outfit and that horse of yours is about the fastest on the place. It was logical. Besides that, the owner said you wasn't worth a hill of beans when it come to fixing fences, and that's what the other boys is doing."

We kept the treatment going every day until the young Appaloosa stopped coming out to meet any approaching rider. Then we ran him and the mares to make sure he'd learned his lesson. He learned to act like a regular range stud. Sometimes it took more to get him corralled with his bunch than the other stud bunches. It was worth it. Nobody got hurt on that place by that horse and he was too good to get rid of because of one defect in character that wasn't his fault.

His spotted colts did have dollar signs on their rumps.

All Tied Up

We'd spent the biggest part of the mornin' corralin' about 1,000 head of steers—yearlin's. It had been pretty tough, the cattle was wild and the country was tough on men an' horses both. Before we got the steers corralled, one hand lost his job an' most of the others felt like quittin'.

Old Ben was fired that day, right on the spot. We'd gathered these yearlings out of a 3,000 acre pasture and they was millin' around in front of the gate to the corrals. We was workin' 'em real easy, inchin' 'em closer and closer and it looked like we could get 'em corralled when Ben, jerkin' down his slicker, hollered and made a rush at the steers just as some was gettin' ready to go into the pen. Ben was goin' as fast as he could through them steers, yellin' as loud as he could and wavin' his slicker over his head. It's a wonder he didn't get bucked off. The end result of his action was 1,000 head of steers scatterin' back into the brush, rocks and greasewood, and Ben sittin' in the corrals without a single critter corralled.

There wasn't much time to do anything but get them steers back before they got into the rough country. Ridin' along side of these steers was sorta like the movies I'd seen, but this wasn't near as romantic.

The cattle ran about half a mile before we got 'em turned and started back towards the corrals again. They were spooked somewhat and we had a time directin' those steers towards where we wanted them. Along the way, the cowboss found Ben and fired him, right then and there.

Finally, we'd got the cattle in the corral and when the gate was latched, everybody took a breather. Horses was tied up and hobbled, chaps and spurs come off and things was made ready to tip them steers.

Trucks were at the corrals ready to haul the steers to the mountain after they were dipped. The work was goin' well and it looked like we might get done pretty close to supper time.

The truckers were loadin' the cattle and the hands were dippin' when one of the truckers called for help. The drivers had pressed the steers too close and they'd knocked down a section of the fence. Steers was pourin' out of the corrals like milk from a spilt bottle. All the hands except them actually dunkin' the cattle ran for their horses. I ran to my horse, untied him and climbed aboard. It felt kinda strange to be ridin' without chaps and spurs but there wasn't time. I started the horse out and figured I had a good chance to head the bunch of escapees.

But the horse didn't respond just right. I was keepin' my eye on the steers and not payin' much attention to my horse. It felt like I was gettin' a buckin' horse ride rather than a smooth flat run. I got after my horse some but it didn't do much good. The other hands passed me even though my horse was doin' his best. He seemed to be workin' pretty hard at it, and I wasn't makin' much progress, so I pulled up, thinkin' something was wrong with my horse.

Something was wrong! I checked the horse all over to see what the problem might be and I couldn't find anything wrong with the horse, The problem was me. I'd forgot to take off the hobbles!

The other hands gathered the loose steers and corralled them although I wasn't much help to them. But we finally got a days work in and I had to give my horse an extra portion of oats 'cause he'd tried his best and yet he was all tied up.

Given' Enough Rope

When l was about 13 or 14, I had the makins of a good hand. I could ride some, I'd been on a buckin' horse or two an' hadn't got throwed too hard anyways. I could rope some and owned all my own equipment.

But this ropin' was something I had yet to master. I was makin' a lot of throws, but not comin' up with much. At this time in my life I wanted to be a calf roper, and the best I could be. I really wanted to dab a rope on a fast runnin' calf, step off a smooth stoppin' horse, run down the rope, throw an' tie the calf, throw up my hands to the cheers of the crowd an' walk away with my pockets full of money. Consequently, I practiced every chance I got.

I roped calves when I could, bales of hay, sagebrush, fence posts, anything. I practiced tiein' down calves when I could, an' the cowdogs when I couldn't. The dogs got wise pretty quick so the only real practice I had was on calves.

When we had cattle to move, I was always prepared. My rope was tied hard and fast to the saddle horn, my horse always had a neck rope on an' my lariat was never tied on with the rope strap. I'd have a loop already built and my rope just sorta hung on the horn. I was prepared for any critter that thought he might want to escape from the herd. I even looked forward to something tryin' to break away as a opportunity for me to improve.

I took a lot of ribbin' from the older hands about my fanatic efforts to rope calves, but I figured it would pay off someday. I kinda made them mad, too! Every now and then, when things slowed down, I'd start swingin' a loop, pick out a likely subject, run thru the herd, rope him and tie him down. During the course of this action, I'd scatter cows, calves an' bulls, an' leave the gatherin' to the other hands. 'Course, before I did something like this, I'd figure it down to where I wouldn't scatter the cattle too bad, but a lot of times I didn't figure too correctly.

I'd get a lot of comments and instruction from the hands when I done this, but a lot of it didn't seem to sink in. One of the comments I heard from an old hand was, "Someday you'll be sorry you're tied hard an' fast. In this country you should learn to dally. I never did figure out what that comment had to do with improvin' my ropin' or keep from scatterin' the herd when I decided to rope one. But I did learn what he meant an' not long afterwards.

We were movin' cattle farther up the mountain. This was good cow country, big sagebrush flats with a lot of grass, broken up by groves of aspen trees that grew along side-hills, a might pretty sight.

As it turned out, we were having a particular problem with one big black baldy cow. She kept wantin' to turn back. We were sure we had her calf somewheres in the herd an' she was sure we didn't. She made a break for it an' got by Dick. I was the next one closest to her an' I took after her, rope wildly swingin'. I heard someone yell, "Get Her Stu!" I wish I knowed who said that.

It occurred to me, as my loop settled over her neck, that I'd have to be careful with the neckrope an' my rope runnin' through it. But I figured if we stayed right behind the cow, we could set her back on her hocks an' I could slip up an' tie her down.

This plan seemed simple enough, except for a few things I forgot or overlooked or neglected to consider.

One of the things I forgot was that this was not ropin' in the rodeo arena for money or fun, this was work. One of the things I overlooked was that this cow was headed towards some mighty big aspen trees. One of the many things I neglected to consider was the fact that I was mounted and in charge of this whole situation.

As things turned out, the cow made it into the trees, and my horse couldn't come to a sharp sliding stop because of the brush and rocks. Through some fancy, fast maneuvering he did find a place to stop, but in doing so, he managed to have a tree between him and the cow.

In that fleeting instant right before the cow hit the end of the rope, I saw the whole picture clearly. I remember thinking how bad that horse's neck and how bad that cow's neck would hurt when this was over. My second thought was how bad my own neck did hurt!

When the cow hit the end of the rope, with a tree between her and the horse, it flipped the horse clear around and laid him on his side. I'd parted company with the horse and hit a tree.

By the time the other hands arrived, the horse had got to his feet, the fight had gone out of the cow an' I was leanin' against a tree analyzin' the situation I'd just lost control of.

We got the cow with the others and put them where we wanted them. My horse held his head kinda strangely for a few days, but then was OK. It took a week or so for me to get around normally and the swelling to go down. It was another week or so before I did any practicing with my rope. However, I didn't practice with a neck rope or tied hard and fast. I started to learn how to dally.

One of the hands asked me what I'd do if the situation happened again. I replied, "I'd turn loose of that rope when she hit the trees, run around the other side, grab the rope, dally an' then proceed to teach the cow a lesson. I've learned enough!"

A Draw

When a feller hires onto a new outfit, he never knows what kind of horses he'll be given to ride. So I was mighty closed-mouthed the first morning we saddled up on the S dot. 'Course, I didn't have much to brag about regarding my bronc riding abilities, anyways.

The horse the cowboss roped out of the cavey for me was a big, rangy blue roan. He looked like a tough horse an' one that could pack a feller anywheres all day long. When I haltered the horse, the cowboss said, "He's a snaffle bit colt an' he ain't been rode for a while."

I says that was okay—I'd buckarooed out in Nevada, an' seen some horses 15 years old or better that never had anything but a snaffle bit in their mouth. But when I bitted him up, I took a look at his teeth—he wasn't a colt by any means!

I got him saddled without any trouble and moved him around some to untrack him before I got on. He had a hump in his back and I really didn't know what I had. So I decided to expect the worst.

The other hands was getting mounted and I didn't want to be last on my first day, so I climbed aboard. I could feel the hump in his back, and very gingerly I touched him with a spur. He stepped out, but he acted like he was walking on eggs and didn't want to bust any. Before we started out, the cowboss says, "Watch him, Stu. He might come undone."

That wasn't necessary, I was staying as close to that saddle as I could!

About a mile or two down the road the horse did come uncorked, and he acted like he didn't care how many eggs was busted. While I managed to stay on him, I don't think any of the hands was too impressed with my bronc riding abilities.

When we started out again, one of the hands rode up alongside me and says, "That ol' pony can be counted on to buck at least once a day…"

I thought to myself, "Well, the worst is over," and started to relax some "…an'," the hand continues, "sometimes he'll buck harder…" that's no problem," I thought. "I rode him and didn't pull leather, and once I learned his pattern of bucking, I might get to scratch his shoulders some an' put on a better show of bronc riding."

"…an' he never bucks the same way twice…" the hand continues.

"Forget scratching his shoulders," I thought. I was relaxing a little more, almost enjoying riding this horse and the other hands conversation.

"…an' sometimes the ol' pony can be counted on to buck twice a day," the hand had finished.

I stopped relaxing, abruptly. The horse didn't do anything bad the rest of the day and I didn't relax any on him.

I used the blue horse every time his turn came up. I especially liked him on long, hard riding days. It seemed like he never would tire out and he could really cover the miles.

As far as my bronc riding ability was concerned, I didn't think I was getting any better. I could ride the horse most of the time, but when he'd give me a new twist, I'd usually get bucked off.

What the hand had said about not bucking the same way twice was absolutely correct. What he didn't say was that the horse would buck anywheres. He'd buck at the home ranch, he'd buck when roping calves or chasing a cow. He even bucked, or tried to, while crossing a river.

The strange part about his bucking was that I never figured out what set him off most of the time. I couldn't figure out if he'd been locoed or was just having fun or if he was really mean.

One time, I was pushing about 30 head of cows and calves down a real steep hill. There was some corrals in the valley below and we were going to wean the calves and haul them to the home ranch. I don't know what started the horse, but he took to bucking, straight down that hill. That was a mighty steep hill and it seemed like for every foot he jumped away from the hill, he'd go down 10. There was a lot of smooth sailing on that bronc ride. He'd jump out and away from the mountain, glide through the air, hit the ground, slide for 10 or 15 feet, then jump out again.

He bucked pretty much straight down that mountain and scattered every cow I'd gathered. Every time we'd sail out through the air, I'd scratch his shoulders some, but I quit that when he almost landed on top of a cow. I was getting some worried about him not keeping his balance and both him and me rolling about 200 yards to the bottom of the mountain.

We made it to the bottom of the mountain, surprisingly with me still on him. Maybe I was too scared to fall off. I'd never been able to tire this horse out before, but he was quivering standing there. I let him catch his breath, then started him back up the mountain to regather my cows.

I guess he wasn't as tired as I thought, maybe he was just scared, because when we got about 10 feet up the mountain he buried his head under his belly, swapped ends and bucked me off, right pronto.

It was a little bit embarrassing, what with all the hands and a few truck drivers watching, but the punchers had seen me ride him before and buck off him before. They were even making bets on the side as to whether the blue or I would win.

I guess, during the year or so I used him, he'd bucked me off about half the time and I'd ride him about half the time. Timeways, he was ahead, because at the end of the day he'd be turned loose to graze, while I had to repair the damages he'd incurred. I don't know how many saddle strings I'd busted, or how many times I loosened my rope strap: I'd pulled it plumb out twice, and once I even had to resew the leather on my saddle horn.

Matched Team

That day, I was sort of embarrassed. I had a job to do and I didn't want to do it. It was an easy enough job, just ride a horse 15 or so miles home and lead another horse. Five or six of those 15 miles were along the highway.

Sometimes I liked to move cows on the highway. I guess I sort of like being in public. A lot of tourists were passing through the country and sometimes they'd stop and talk with you, take your picture and the like. And sometimes there would be a pretty girl stop and talk a while. I didn't mind the stopping and talking and I even kind of enjoyed the posing for pictures. A lot of times it made for a lot of fun.

But today I wasn't looking forward to this job. I had been selected to catch a team of work horses, ride one and lead the other back to the main ranch. I wanted to take a truck and haul them back, but the trucks were either in use or broken-down. The reason I was selected for this job was because I was the cowboy.

This outfit I was working on was a sheep ranch. They had about 150 head of cows. It was my job to look after the cows, mess with a few colts, hunt some lost sheep and do some of these odd jobs, like bringing a team of horses home. It was pretty good job except for some of these humiliating experiences that kept cropping up.

I was driven to the pasture where the team was kept. I had my saddle, saddle blankets, a halter, my snaffle bit, a bucket of grain and a bridle that went to the harness that fit the team. I'd thrown it in just in case my bridle wouldn't let out large enough to fit one of these horses.

The team answered the sound of the horn honking and came on the run. Big as they were, they weren't running fast, but they made an impressive sight. They were big horses, weighed about 1,800 pounds each. Matched greys. A feller would have thought he was seeing double.

I really envied those horses. They were only used during the summer to move a sheep camp every so often, then turned out on good pasture. During the winter, they only saw about three months work, pulling a hay wagon. Consequently, they stayed fat and slick.

I'd been told that one of these horses was broke to ride. But they looked exactly alike and I had a hard time remembering which one was the horse I was supposed to ride and which one I was supposed to lead.

The mare acted a little more snorty than the gelding, so I put my saddle on the gelding. I knew that saddle didn't fit, but I had plenty of saddle blankets and I figured it wouldn't hurt him too much to carry it home at a walk. I had to let the cinches out as far as they would go to get all the straps adjusted right. My own snaffle bit and headstall wouldn't fit the gelding, so I had to use the harness bridle that belonged to the horse, complete with blinders and 15 feet of driving lines.

I got the halter on the mare, untracked the gelding and climbed aboard. I wasn't surprised when the gelding started to buck. In fact, I'd half expected it. He hadn't been used for a couple of months and he was feeling pretty good. What surprised me was how good a job of bucking he was doing. He was hitting the ground with every ounce of that 1,800 pounds. If anybody had been watching, they'd have thought I was pulling leather because I had the mare dallied up. But I managed to stay on and the mare stayed right alongside, just like she was used to being there.

Before long I got the gelding stopped, but not before I felt like he'd jarred every bone in my body. I was sore! And I was awful glad that the gelding hadn't bucked harder.

The ride down the canyon was uneventful, except for me thinking how lucky I was that I'd picked the broke horse to ride home and how fortunate I was that the mare was used to working on the right side. If she'd have wanted to stay on the left side I'd have had to turn her loose or be drug off the gelding by the lead shank while he was bucking.

I tried to hurry the horses along when we hit the highway. It was embarrassing to be seen riding a work horse, complete with blinders and lines, in public. I kept my head down and hoped none of the local folks would recognize me. I was really glad that no tourists stopped and asked for pictures. They have a way of catching a feller without his best horse, taking his picture, then labeling the photo "Cowboy with his favorite horse" or something like that. Humiliating to say the least.

When I rode into the yard at the ranch, the boss had a grin on his face. I guess we did look a little funny, blinders and all.

"Don't you know the difference between a mare and a gelding?" He asked.

"Of course I know the difference," I replied as I unsaddled the horse.

"Well," said the boss, still grinning, "I told you that the mare was broke to ride."

Now I did not want to admit that I had just plumb forgot what he said, so I told him, as nonchalantly as possible, "Now you've really got a matched team, 'cause the gelding is broke to ride too!"

Excuses

There's more than one way to get off a horse. The first way–the one we all like–is simple, just swing a leg over and put it on level ground. That's easy enough, once a person has mastered it. But I've seen plenty of people who couldn't even do that gracefully. Oft times they would get a foot down and then just fall, flat on their backs or elsewhere.

Then a feller could always get a little help from the horse–like getting bucked off. That's happened to me plenty of times. When I was younger, I used to keep track of how many times I'd been bucked off by punching a new hole in my belt. I figured I was doing pretty good until one day I had to buy a new belt! I'd still have that old belt today if I'd have just punched a new hole in it every time I rode a horse!

Sometimes a rider can just become separated from his horse, like when the horse goes left and the rider was thinking right. This can happen going around a tree or sagebrush, cutting cattle or almost anything else.

But is it possible for anyone to just plumb fall off a horse, and not have any excuse as to what the horse did wrong? Before I'd have said no there are too many excuses for becoming separated from a horse unintentionally–he bucked, or moved, or "I wanted to get off and he helped me," or there was a horsefly on his neck. There are plenty of excuses no matter how watered down they may seem. But can anyone just fall off a horse?

Yes! Surely! And that's a fact! I know people can just fall off horses because I did it myself. And the horse didn't help me any either, I did it all by myself.

The way this came about was that after a lifetime of chasing cows for somebody else, I decided to borrow $25,000 and buy me a two-bit, one horse outfit of my own. I borrowed enough money to buy a few cows and saved up enough to buy a horse.

Now this little horse I bought was started but not broke. I had enough riding to get him going real good, but not enough to make a good horse out of him. So I hired out to the neighbors on weekends, holidays, vacation or whenever I could get away, just to give the horse as much riding and experience as I could give him. Soon he started to really take to a cow and it wasn't long before I started to rope off him. The horse really seemed to take an interest in working cows. And he was doing a lot of it on his own.

The day I just plumb fell off this horse wasn't his fault, it was mine. I had 15 or 20 cows with late calves, some yearlings and an extra bull or two to move to the river for the summer. In this bunch of cattle, I had one calf yet to brand and I wanted to do it before we moved the cows.

We'd planned to move these cattle on a Saturday afternoon, after I'd done some errands in town. My wife, being somewhat impatient, couldn't wait until I got home to brand the calf. On foot she gathered the cattle from the small pasture by the house, put them in the corral and caught my horse. While she was waiting for me, I was waiting in line in the grocery store picking up some items for her. I'd told her the reason I wanted the cows in the corral was to catch the calf and brand him. She forgot.

When I didn't show up on time, she and the kids started the cattle down the road. She had the kids go ahead of the cattle and block off the neighbors' roadways and gardens. Being eight months pregnant, she thought it would be better to walk than to ride the horse. So when I showed up at the house, there wasn't a cow, wife or kid in sight, just the horse tied up in the corral.

The first thing that came to my mind was that my $25,000 banker had decided to foreclose on my two-bit operation. After a mile or two search, I found my cows and my family. The kids were watching the crossroads and gardens and my wife was bringing up the rear, bossing the whole works, just like she always did.

We had the kids hold the cattle while my wife and I went back to the house to get the branding irons and a gas bottle to brand the calf. I saddled the horse and rode him to where the kids were holding the cattle. My wife drove the truck.

We started the cattle again, and this time my wife drove the kids ahead of the cattle and dropped them off in front of the driveways and gardens. The kids sure liked to see that pickup, rather than walk up to each drive-way. We made a pretty rag-tag outfit going up the road.

When we finally got out in the open where we didn't have to watch open gates and the like, I loaded the kids in the truck and took down my rope. Right along here would be as good as any place to brand the calf.

I debated on whether or not to make a fire and get the irons hot, but finally decided not to. I'm not a great roper and it might be a mile or two up the road before I caught the calf.

I was having second thoughts about not building the fire when I laid my first loop down, pretty as a picture, and that calf put both hind feet in it. I figured myself quite the roper, even though I was somewhat surprised.

In making such a beautiful catch, I'd let out too much rope. No problem, I thought I'd just raise up a little on the saddle and make this catch complete. My little horse was doing just what I wanted him to do, following the calf. Maybe he was doing too good a job because when the calf went off the road down into the barrow pit, the horse followed. I'd let more of my rope out than I'd thought and was raising higher and higher out of the saddle. I was even leaning back and to the left with my right arm as high as I could get it.

Now when that little horse went down into that barrow pit, I was in somewhat of a precarious position. But not for long, because the next thing I knew, I was on the ground.

I still had a hold of my rope and still had my calf caught with the rope stretched across the saddle. My horse was standing there, looking back at me as if to say, "Cut the monkey business and let's get this job done."

I got the calf branded, among the jeering of my wife and the kids. As we continued up the road, I analyzed the situation. I hadn't gotten off intentionally and the horse hadn't bucked me off–he'd just walked out from under me. I plain fell off!

How Much Is A Mule Worth?

The cows was pretty well taken care of, they didn't need much supervision. Other than changin' pasture now and then, pickin' up some strays, and makin' sure the water troughs were runnin', there really wasn't much ridin' to do. When us cowboys were approached by the superintendent of this outfit to help with some of the other chores, we were pretty handy at figgurin' out something else that just had to be done, from horseback of course, an' it needed our immediate attention. But one day, we ran out of plausible excuses. We were selected by the super to go to the mountain an' load some poles that had already been cut an' limbed for a new set of corrals that was being built.

We'd managed to keep out of the posthole diggin' end of this project, but today we were caught. The super told us that the poles were already cut, most of them stacked pretty close to the road.

"Why," said the super. "You won't even need your horses, just throw em' on the trucks and trailers." It sounded pretty easy, but I still had some misgivings. It still sounded like work to me. Now, I'd always wanted one of them jobs where I didn't have to do much, but I got paid a lot of money for it. And I'm sure some of my former employers would say that I'd had just that when I'd worked for them. An' I'd probably still be workin' for some of them, I think, if I'd have been paid more. I figured I'd reached that degree of professionalism where if I couldn't do it from horseback, somebody else could do it or it didn't really need bein' done.

This outfit paid by the hour, the first time I'd ever worked cows on an hourly basis, an' I was already figgurin' that there was a lot of other things wrong with this job as we were drivin' up the mountain. When we got to where the poles were cut, we found out that the super was right. There was some poles stacked right next to the road—about 40. What we had come for was about 500! The more I thought about it the worse I liked it. But they was nice poles, 20 to 22 feet long.

I knew I wasn't goin' to like this, but I figured I would dislike it less if I didn't have to do it long. So I started right in draggin' poles up to the road an' loadin' 'em in the trailer. I never have quite figured out why, on a project such as this, the poles were always cut on the downhill side of the road. It was an uphill drag all the way. After about four trips, I took off my spurs. It was the first time they'd been off them boots for probably six or eight months. But it didn't make much difference, I was stumblin' and trippin' just as much with them off as I was with them on.

I wasn't enjoyin' this job an' I got to figurin' that I'd feel alot better when I was done than I did while I was doin' it. Them other fellers, I guess they liked it. It seemed to me that they liked it, enjoyed it, an' wanted it to last a long time, and were perfectly willing to do anything to let just that happen. I guess that's why I was gettin' three poles up to the trailers to every one of theirs.

It took long enough to get the trailers and trucks loaded an' I was sure glad when we got done. The other fellers looked sorta relieved when we got done, not disappointed as I thought they might. We got the poles back to where they was buildin' the corrals, an' I immediately started thinkin' of excuses I might use so as I wouldn't get in on the nailin' end of this project.

We did have some ridin' to do for a few days, then I was called into the super's office. He told me that the foreman had mentioned that I had really worked my tail off getin' them poles.

I told him I had an' that the next time I was goin' to be a little more careful. Being a skinny cowboy, I didn't have much to spare. But he must have been appreciative because he gave me a twenty-five cent an hour raise. I did some quick figurin' and come to the conclusion that on some days that would be worth three dollars an others it wouldn't be worth a cup of coffee. But I thanked him an' asked him how the corrals was coming—just out of courtesy.

He said they hadn't started nailin' up poles yet, but figured the corrals would be done by fall so as we could ship calves an' use them for that sorta stuff.

Now this was a pretty big outfit I was workin' on. In addition to runnin' about 1500 head of cattle an' growin' hay to feed them in the winter, they ran a motel and convention center, gas station, boat marina and restaurant. They even had a place where the tourists could rent a horse an' take a ride for an hour or two. And they had a team of mules that they hooked up to a wagon now an' then to give some of the tourists a ride.

I didn't get in on any of this tourist trade an' was mighty glad of it. The feller that was runnin' the horse end of it was always complainin' that in addition to takin' care of the horses, he had to fix the plumbin' and help with repairs in the restaurant when needed. But he did keep the horses an' mules in good shape an' I admired how fat an' slick an' sassy they looked as I drove past them on my way back to the cow camp. I got to thinkin' how nice it would have been to have had those mules to snake those poles up to the trailers, rather than me doin' it. It might have meant that I wouldn't have got the two-bit an hour raise, but not knowin' about it, I wouldn't have missed it.

About a week later, us cowboys got a call from the super. We was needed to go to the mountain an' haul some more poles down. And, much to my dismay, he asked specifically for me. I thought that they had decided to enlarge the original plan for the corrals, but I really saw red when I heard what happened to the first bunch of poles we hauled down.

The posts for the corrals were set 8 feet apart an' rather than usin' 16 or 17 feet of each pole, makin' it span two posts, somebody come along an' cut a 10 foot section right out of the middle of each pole, leavin' a worthless 6 or 7 foot length of pole on the ground. Now if I'd have been doin' it, I'd have done it so as I used the whole pole an' if some had to be trimmed, I could trim it an' have it come out fireplace size. I ain't exactly lazy: I'd rather say I am sorta conservative, because I don't like to do things twice. But the way they done it, somebody was havin' to go to the mountain to get more poles an' somebody was goin' to have to cut the wasted ends to fireplace size.

I sure wasn't anxious to go up an' work my tail off again, so I started figurin' out how to get out of this project. Then I thought of those fat, sleek mules that wasn't hardly earnin' their keep.

We commandeered the mules an' their harnesses before the sun come up the morning we went to get the poles. I was in better spirits; I'd already figured it out so as I wouldn't have to do much. I'd convinced the foreman that he should bring his horse, then he could lead a mule as they snaked out the poles... that would be a lot easier than walkin'. I also convinced him that a few extra hands to load the poles an' a few extra hands to snag 'em an' hook 'em to the singletree was a good idea.

I was almost lookin' forward to this trip even though I became the butt of some asinine jokes from the other hands because of the mules. I hadn't worked much with mules before, but I'd heard lots of fellers tell about how good they was to work with, how they'd outwork a horse an' how they was smarter than a horse. Now I'd been around horses all my life an' it sorta bothered me how many of them was smarter than me. I was a little apprehensive that these mules might be smarter than those horses an' kinda concerned that they might be smart enough to where I would end up doin' a lot of work! I'd also heard how they kicked hard an' always aimed before they kicked. If that was an indication that horses didn't aim when they kicked, I didn't want anything to do with the mules.

But it didn't work that way. It seems like everyone forgot how a harness fits—everyone except me. I found myself nervously harnessin' a team of mules, for the first time. But everything went all right an' them mules turned out to be plumb gentle.

We had quite a discussion on what to call the mules, we didn't know their names. We decided to call the gelding SIR an' the mare LADY. We also had quite a discussion as to what to call a female mule. To this day I still don't know whether to call them mares, jennys, or what! Some other suggestions was given as to what to call the female mule, but as soon as everybody saw how well-mannered she was an' how good she worked, the name LADY stuck.

We worked each mule for a half-load of poles. I took a lot of pleasure in watchin' those mules snake those poles up the hill. I'd thought of the idea an' saved myself some hard work. I was sorta proud too, that it took a team of mules to replace me. And, I'd even got a raise in pay out of the situation.

I decided not to brag about the situation too much though. Being replaced by two mules might give everybody a double opportunity to make more of those asinine jokes about me!

Still Wet Behind The Ears

It started out to be a pretty good kind of a day. The sun was just coming up and there wasn't a cloud in the sky. As I pulled my boots on, I thought that they might make it 'til fall. There were holes in both of them and I was wearing heavy socks to help patch them up. There was also a big hole in the crown of my hat, about the size of a silver dollar. I figured when I hit town in the fall I could get some new clothes, starting at the top and not stopping 'til I hit the bottom.

As I strapped on my chink chaps, I figured at least I'd be cool, what with all the holes in my clothing. What we had to do today was going to be hot work. We had to take about a hundred head of cows with the bigger calves and push them to the top of Sam's Canyon. It would be a hot day, but there was a lot of good feed going to waste and we wanted to use it. Water would be a problem, but somebody had carved a road out of the side of the mountain, hauled up some cement, a new granary, plastic pipe and some water troughs.

They constructed a guzzler, or catchment, as they called it. They poured a cement pad about the size of a football field on a slope above where they set the granary. They designed it so that the snow melt and rain-water would funnel into the granary.

From the bottom of the granary, they hooked up the pipe and ran a line about four miles long, and put a water trough into the pipe every mile or so. By putting a float on each trough and using the pressure of the water in the pipe, we could keep each trough full all the time.

If we salted pretty close to the troughs, we could keep the cattle on top as long as the feed and the water held out.

We made a good gather without much trouble. Gordon had to rope a big cow with foot rot and before anyone could make a heel catch on her, she was headed right to the middle of a good sized lake. Gordon was having trouble with his dallies and had to follow the cow into the lake. His horse stepped over the rope a couple of times and had himself pretty well wrapped up. Gordon didn't have any choice but to let his rope and the cow go.

The rope worked itself free when Gordon turned it loose and it's a good thing that it did. Both Gordon and his horse could have been drowned if he hadn't. I got the cow caught when she climbed out on the other side of the lake, and someone else heeled her.

We had the cow stretched out, doctored, all the ropes off and turned loose before Gordon got out of the lake. He was wet all over and he sloshed when he walked. As he coiled his rope, he was mighty careful to pick the moss off it.

He emptied his boots and tied them on his saddle, then he took off his socks and hung them on the swells to dry. He wasn't much help sorting pairs because he was particular about where he rode without his boots and socks.

We got what cows and calves we needed, gave them a chance to mother up and started for the top of Sam's Canyon. We knew it would be easier going if the calves started out with their moms.

We took our time heading up the mountain, just poking along. We had a long way to go and there wasn't any rush. Every now and then one of the hands would take down a rope and practice heeling some calves, just to relieve the boredom.

Clouds had built up off to the west and a slight breeze had started up . I remember thinking that this was what we needed to cool off a hot afternoon. As the day wore on, the clouds kept getting darker and darker, and the wind got cooler and cooler. The hands that had them put on jackets.

When we reached the steep part of the trail we began breaking the herd up into smaller bunches of 25 or 30 head, what one man could handle good and keep the herd moving up the hill.

We were almost at the top with the first bunch when the storm hit. The hail came first. The hailstones were as big as good sized marbles. They came with a pounding, driving force that made the cows turn tail to drift with the storm. The horses held their heads way down low. There wasn't really a man or critter that wanted to be there. When the hail stopped, the rain hit fast and furious. It wasn't long before everyone was soaked. My chaps were soaked clear through.

We managed to fight the cows through the rain to the top of the mountain and put them on water. Some of the hands remarked that it was silly to worry about putting cows on the water seeing as they had to swim to the top of the mountain. There were some jokes about how the cow boss and Noah might even up in some sort of contest. We finally came to the conclusion that Noah would win. The cow boss had overlooked building a boat. The boys were trying to make the best of a bad situation.

We'd planned on holding the cattle on top for a few hours and giving the calves a chance to mother up, but we came up the mountain so slow, most of the calves were with their moms already. Most of the men were cold and wet already.

One of them was complaining about how miserable he was. He wanted to register a complaint with the cow boss. He said he'd never seen anything like this in the movies or on TV!

Gordon wasn't fairing too well. This was the second time he'd gotten wet today and he was saying that he was getting "wetter in more areas than he did earlier."

I wasn't doing much good either. Some of the hands were remarking that with the holes in my boots and the holes in my hat, the water was running clear through! That's exactly how I felt. Being a skinny little cowboy, there sure wasn't much to slow the water up.

Some of the new hands that were a little green got some good experience. Getting wet behind the ears helped them. I felt like I got some good experience, too.

In addition to buying new boots and a new hat when I hit town, I also bought a new slicker. Getting wet behind the ears was no fun.

The Critic

When a feller gets married and the kids start coming along, sometimes he has second thoughts about forking broncs on a regular basis. So it was with me, I decided to quit rodeoing. I figured I could handle what bronc riding I had to do on the ranch, but I wasn't going out traveling, looking for broncs to ride.

I was sorta relieved to know that the sudden meetings with the ground might come to an end and really pleased to know that this bone or that bone wasn't going to be broke. As a bronc rider, I knew I wasn't as good as I wanted to be anyway and although I hated to admit it, I was getting older.

Now I could talk up a pretty good bronc ride and my kids got to the point where they all had my bronc riding stories memorized. I didn't have too many to tell them, 'cause I only told the stories where I rode the horse and made some money. Some stories weren't too long, 'cause if I got bucked off, I never told the end of the story. Like the one where I was at a rodeo in eastern Utah.

I was single then, and kinda thought I could ride anything with hair on it. I was quite a bit more reckless than I am now. I'd entered the bareback bronc riding but couldn't get entered in saddlebronc. I always figured my chances of taking home some money was better if I entered more than one event.

As it turned out, there was a big gray horse in this bucking string and he was known to be a chute-fighting son-of-a-gun that knew every dirty trick in the book and spent his spare time trying to invent new ones. The fellow that drawed this horse? Well, his wife was in the grandstand. When she saw how much trouble her husband was having just getting his saddle on, she came down and put a fast stop on his bronc riding for that day.

It was too late to get entered, but I told the chute boss that for money, "I'd ride that old gray nag out." I pocketed a $10 bill and, after some fighting, cussing and a rough time in general, I got my saddle on the bronc. After some more fighting, I managed to mount. As soon as I found my stirrups, I asked for the gate and that horse never hesitated. He came out sun-fishing, fighting mad and really turning on the crank.

That's about as much as I'd tell the kids, other than to describe in a little more detail how hard he bucked. I know how hard he bucked 'cause I spent most of the time on the ground, watching him buck. I never did tell the kids he bucked me off shortly after they opened the gate. Very shortly.

The kids spent most of the time in town with their mother, and it looked like they might never see their old man ride a bucking horse.

One day they came out for a visit. I had some horses in the corral and each one of the kids had a chance for a ride. Among the horses in the corral was a little black horse with a blaze face and four white stocking feet.

I'd bought him mostly because he was kinda good looking and I figured my kids might win some 4-H contests with him. I hadn't used him much. He'd come up lame so I just turned him out. He was still pretty green.

I figured the riding wouldn't hurt him and the kids might enjoy seeing him rode. I got him saddled and stepped on him in the round corral. The kids were sitting on the fence watching me warm him up wanting to have their turns at him.

Now I don't know what set this little horse off, but something surely did and he started into bucking, squealing and trying to paw the earth apart. This little horse couldn't buck hard, but he was giving it a good try. The kids were on the fence enjoying the little rodeo.

After the initial surprise of the horse bucking wore off, I kinda relaxed and started to enjoy the rodeo myself. It had been a few years since I'd rode anything that bucked.

I started laughing when I heard one of the kids encouraging the horse. I laughed quite a bit more when I thought how silly I'd look in front of my kids if this little horse did buck me off. I was laughing hard enough that I blowed a stirrup. This was getting serious, but I couldn't stop laughing . I was getting a little looser in the saddle every jump, but I couldn't stop laughing.

I did manage to get his head pulled up and stopped before he bucked me off. I realized that this was the first time any of the kids had seen their old man on a bucking horse and decided to do a little bragging on myself.

I asked each kid what they thought of their old man as a bronc rider. My daughter, Chris, thought it was OK, but then girls didn't really think much about bronc riding. Sam and Ben, being the youngest, did get a little excited. Sam admitted to encouraging the horse. They both thought it was neat.

Willie was probably the most honest and took the winds out of my sails when I asked him what he'd thought of his old man as a bucking horse rider. His answer was pretty simple and straight forward: "Aw, dad, he didn't buck very hard!"

Easy Calvin'–
It's Not Like The Old Days

There was a loud crash before the light came on. My wife bolted upright in bed, and caught me red-handed, holding what I had thought was her blow dryer.

"What's going on here?" I could tell by her tone that she was somewhat upset.

"I just wanted to get your blow dryer," I answered meekly. "Remember when we dried off that calf last year with it? Well, we got another one that needs some help."

"Well, what are you doing with that at three in the morning?"

I looked down at my hand. What I had certainly wasn't a blow dryer, at least as I remembered blow dryers. Actually, I didn't know what I had.

"Where is the blow dryer?" I inquired testily. "And what is this thing?"

"That," she replied, "is a curling iron. My blow dryer is in the kitchen. I had to use it to defrost the ice box. Now put the curling iron away; it's too late to give that new calf a permanent."

I went to the kitchen to get the blow dryer, muttering something about never putting equipment back where it belongs. The blow dryer was right next to the coffee maker.

I guess it won't hurt just this once, I thought, as I put the blow dryer, coffee maker, coffee, a cup, a spoon, some sugar and cream in a sack. Besides, it's wet and kinda cold, and I might be up all night.

That was three weeks ago. Just the other day, I was again caught red-handed.

"Where in the world are you going with that?" My wife wanted to know.

"Down to the calving barn," I answered. Obviously, she had seen that I had the color T.V. on the hay wagon, next to the AC-DC welder.

"I might be convinced that you need the welder down there, but why the television?"

I patiently explained that I needed the welder as an additional source of power since I had blown a fuse the previous night. Also, three or four heifers were almost ready to calve and I didn't want to take any chances on falling asleep.

"The T.V.," I pointed out, "will help keep me awake. Besides, I wanted to watch the rest of that movie and catch the late news." I thought that might satisfy her curiosity and it sure sounded logical to me, which just shows how wrong I can be sometimes.

"You'll catch more than the news if you keep hauling my house down to your corrals." She eyed me menacingly.

"Good Lord! You've already got my blow dryer, my coffee maker, the toaster, an electric can opener, the microwave oven, an electric blanket, the alarm clock and a radio, not to mention every extension cord in the house. Now you want the television. I'm about ready to blow a fuse, too!"

She turned toward the house, muttering something about "next it will be the front room furniture."

In fact, I had considered taking my easy chair out of the front room; but now, sensing her angry mood, I decided to wait a couple of days.

Yes, the days of bringing weak or chilled calves into the kitchen, drying them off with gunny sacks and finding a place for them behind the stove are over. Thanks to the wonders of modern technology and electricity, muddy boots in the kitchen are a thing of the past.

Now if I hung some pictures on the corral posts and scraped some of the corral dust into a corner and did some straightening up maybe, just maybe, my wife would come down to the calving barn and visit me next calving season. After all, even she would have to admit it really is quite comfortable. It has all the comforts of home.

The VCR

I got a date. Don't know how I did it, but I got a date, an' she was a big rodeo fan to boot! She'd told me she had even tried a few bareback broncs in some girl's rodeos.

Now this was just what an older bull rider like myself needed to put a little spark in his life, an' I started plannin' out my date. I figured we'd have some dinner at a pretty fancy restaurant. Really do it up right.

Then, because she was a big rodeo fan an' a competitor also, I thought I'd run her over to a friend's house an' watch his VCR. He'd taken some VCR pictures at the local county fair and rodeo just a few weeks earlier an' even had some of me on my bull. I hadn't seen them yet an' was anxious to see if I could tell what happened. The bull I'd drawed had throwed me pretty hard an' I still wasn't sure why, what, how or even when.

After that I thought we might do a little dancin' at a local honky-tonk.

The evening went pretty well. Supper at the fancy restaurant was mighty good although some of the other customers might have thought we were dressed inappropriately in our Levis.

The VCR show went pretty good an' the gal really took an interest in the bareback broncs. We skipped over the timed events, lingered over the saddle broncs an' went directly to the bulls.

I know most of the bulls in this string an' most of the bull riders, so we spent a lot of time runnin' this part of the tape in slow motion.

My ride was the last one on the tape an' when we got to it, my friend run it over five or six times.

Suddenly my date got up an' started to put on her coat. "What's wrong?" I asked.

"Time to go," she said.

"How come?"

"Well, we could sit here all night watchin' that tape, an' that fool still ain't goin' to get that bull rode!"

We left to go dancin' an' I was sorta relieved to know that she didn't recognize "that fool".

Or did she?

Courteous Horse

The little dark chestnut filly was just as nice a horse as a feller could want; some white markings kinda high up on all four legs an' a white strip down her face added a touch of class and accented her action. Conformation wise, I couldn't fault her, although she could have been a little bigger. But she was big enough to carry a skinny, old cowboy like myself all day.

The people that owned her allowed a neighbor girl to take care of her an' she did a fine job with the horse. That gal kept the horse brushed down an' slicked up all the time. The girl also broke an' trained the filly an' she did a fine job there too! Not only was the filly nice to look at, but she was well mannered. As a matter of fact, the mare was more of a pet than anything else.

I inquired as to how much the owner might take for the horse, an' his price was high enough that I knew he didn't want to sell the horse very bad. The thought of owning a well mannered horse that would come when called just sorta excited me. I had plenty of horses, mostly colts, but even the older horses I had were still kinda broncs, an' they were all hard to catch. I just didn't have the time to teach these horses some real manners, although they were all good horses, an' most of them had a lot of cow savvy. They all were rode regular an' when the day's work was done, they were turned loose, but they didn't have any of the little courtesies this mare had.

I approached the owner again about selling the horse an' he confessed that he didn't really want to sell her, in fact, he was convinced the filly really had promise an' was goin' to send her to a professional horse trainer for some real "high school" type education. I told him that I thought the girl had done a whale of a job on the filly an' that while some professional training might help, all the filly really needed was more work, rather than just ridin' up an' down the road—after all, that gets kinda boring for both the horse an' rider.

He allowed as that was right, but he wanted the filly to be something special so she was going to a special horse trainer.

I'd forgot about the whole thing an' was surprised two or three months later when I saw the owner of the filly in the cafe. He asked me if I was still interested in the horse because he'd thought about selling her.

I was immediately interested again in the horse. He told me what he'd take for the filly, an' even though it was more than I wanted to pay, I got to thinkin' she'd sure be worth it.

I told him I'd like to try her in the mountains for a week or two before I bought her. To my knowledge, she'd never been in the mountains an' I just wanted to see how she handled herself in the rocks an' amongst the trees. He got a funny look on his face, but agreed.

I had some cows to move on the mountain the following week an' just couldn't wait to take her an' try her after the cattle. In fact, I couldn't wait so bad, that I rode her out to do my irrigatin' the next day when we got her over to my place. It was a real pleasure even though I didn't like to irrigate. The filly was real smooth to ride an' I could turn her loose while I did my work an' she'd just follow me around. My own horses, I had to tie them up or hobble them, then sometimes I'd have a tough time what with the shovel an' wet, slick irrigatin' boots.

I hauled her up on the mountain a few days later. I jingled in my horses, they were all fat an' slick. I got to thinkin' how nice it would be if some of them were as courteous as this little mare.

I made some coffee in camp while I waited for the other members of the grazing association to show up. We had a lot of cattle to move an' everyone was goin' to pitch in.

When everyone arrived an' we'd had all the coffee we wanted it was time to get started. I had slipped the bridle off the filly, just turned her loose, an' thought I would impress everyone by just callin' her an' have her come to me. I did, she did an' everyone was impressed. They were all familiar with some of the kinds of horses I had.

We started out, single file, to move cows. The mare sorta stumbled over a log that was layin' across the trail, but I pulled her head up an' we continued on. That was the purpose of havin' her up there, to see how she handled herself. We went on an' I didn't think much of it, except that I noticed she seemed to stumble a lot, and once or twice I thought she might be goin' down. Then suddenly, I found out why she seemed to stumble a lot.

We'd been out a couple of hours, had some cattle gathered an' were really getin' into our work. An old cow decided she didn't want to make this journey with us an' tried to quit the bunch. The little mare an' me took off after her in hot pursuit.

We hadn't gone 20 yards, had a log to cross, an' I thought she'd just jump it.

She did, I'm not sure what happened next, but I felt the filly goin' down an' couldn't stop her. I was throwed right over her head an' sorta rolled up to an Aspen tree. The action had attracted a crowd.

"You alright Stu?"

"Yep," I said as I untangled myself from the tree. "But what's wrong with my horse?"

The mare was in a funny position. She was down on one knee, with the other front leg stretched out in front of her. Her head was tucked between her front legs. I was sure she had tangled herself in the reins, but she wasn't fightin' or strugglin' any. Then I thought that she had busted something.

"Ain't nothin' wrong with your horse," somebody said, "other than she has just throwed you an' is takin' a bow for it! If we give her a round of applause, she'll probably straighten right up."

The filly did look like she was takin' a bow, and when everyone started clappin' she got up on all fours. She really looked quite pleased with herself.

I straightened the saddle an' someone asked me, "What does she do for an encore?" I didn't find that at all funny, but everyone else seemed to enjoy it.

We continued with our cow work an' I took a lot of teasin' about my horse bein' so courteous. However, I was gettin' an education of my own. I noticed that every time a good-sized branch brushed her alongside the knees, she started to "bow". I thought she had been stumblin' all day, but she had only been tryin' to perform as trained… I figured out what a "high-schooled" horse was.

I decided that I really didn't need a trick horse or one that had more education than l did, so I returned her to her owner. Along with the filly, I took one of my best colts an' left him at the gal's place who had taught the filly such nice manners. I was goin' to have me a courteous horse, I but I didn't need a high-schooled horse.

Moonlight Ride

I first met Albert Taylor when I was working on Owen Barton's Diamond A Ranch on the Idaho-Nevada border.

Albert lived in an old log cabin a few miles away from the ranch. I don't know how he made his living, other than tradin' a few horses, but his wants were simple and he didn't need much cash.

He didn't own a car, he did all his travelling horseback. If he did have to go into town for some reason, he'd ride his horse to the ranch and have Owen drive him into town.

I always liked to see Al ride into the ranch. Always chewing gum, Al was, and he was always ready to tell some stories about when he was younger, and ridin' the rough string.

As he rode into the ranch this day, I was hoping to get him to tell my favorite story. Coming right out and asking him to tell a story was a sure-fire way to get him to "clam up," so I figured I'd have to be pretty tricky about getting him to open up.

"We're headin' towards the Jones place today, Al. Anything interestin' ever happen down there?" Al was getting off his horse as I asked the question.

"Well," says Al, "that used to be great horse country down there. Mustangs was runnin' all over. But you heard that before, didn't you, Stu?"

"Yep," I says. I had to get all the circumstances right to get Al to tell me this story. "I guess with all them horses, there was some good bronc riders in those days."

"Yes sir, Stu, there sure was. Them boys, and me too, we used to ride 'em till they quit, and sometimes they'd keep it up all day and all night."

Al was quiet for quite a while and I got to thinkin' maybe I tried a little too hard to get him talkin'. The old feller may have been a little more sensitive than I thought. But pretty soon, he opened up.

"Stu, sometimes a feller has to ride like his life depended on it and it don't make no difference whether it's night or day. I remember," continued Al, "when I was sixteen or seventeen, them guys that had the Jones place was a wild bunch, rough ridin' bronc riders, hard drinkers, and just plain reckless. They was rough and tough, and didn't care to be put down by men or horses."

"On this particular occasion," said Al, "they was comin' in from town, all mounted on their best horses and pretty well liquored up, when they run into a bunch of mustangs. They knew the horses, they'd run 'em before, without success. But they decided to try 'em again."

Al then told me how he was out hunting for strays and happened to see how them fellers run them horses in. He said they never would have caught them horses if the feller who was tryin' to turn 'em hadn't of fell off his horse when the horse fell. The feller stood up and that was all that was needed to spook them horses into the wings that led into a horse trap. He figured they'd probably had more to drink than they thought they did, 'cause they'd of never caught them horses if they didn't.

"After them horses was corraled," continued Al, "they broke out another bottle and decided who was going to ride the big roan stud who bossed the bunch. The feller that finally won the right to ride the stud was a mighty good bronc rider. I think his name was Dick Grey. Somebody roped the big roan and snubbed him while Dick saddled him up. Dick climbed in the saddle, and before he could ask for the gate, someone tied his feet together, under the horse! Then when he asked for the horse, the snubber, rather than giving the reins to Dick, reached up and pulled the complete hackamore off the horse."

"Course," says Al, "the second that roan stud was free, he started buckin', he almost bucked right over the snubber and his horse. Well Dick was doin' a right good job of ridin' that horse, but he probably didn't even know his feet was tied together under the horse when he hollered, 'Open the gate!'"

The roan headed straight for the gate when it was open and a few of the hands jumped their own horses and run right along side of Dick and the roan, yellin' and hollerin' encouragement to both Dick and the roan. But pretty soon, after a couple of hundred yards, the riders started peelin' off, leaving Dick by himself, on the roan."

Al told me that he was invited by the Jones boys to spend the night, which he did. He said that just before everyone turned in, and Dick Grey hadn't returned, someone asked the boss if they shouldn't go out and look for Dick. "No", says the boss, "Dick can take care of himself," and with that, they all turned in.

The next mornin' when the hands was saddlin' their gentlest horses, Dick showed up! Yep, he was still horseback, his feet was tied underneath the horse, and he had that horse broke to neck-rein, in a fashion.

Every time Dick wanted to turn the horse, he'd slap him alongside the neck. If he slapped him on the right side, the horse would turn left, and vice-versa. Dick brought the horse in, almost broke, safe and sound, both him and the horse. Dick got loose from the horse when someone found a pocket knife and cut him loose.

"He sure made a bronc ride that night," said Al, "and he turned out to be the best reinin' horse on the outfit. So, Stu, if you think you are a top notch bronc rider try doin' that some night!"

"No thanks, Al," I said, "but I'll bet you another pack of smokes I can roll me a smoke while ridin' this horse buckin'." The horse I was ridin' this day would usually buck a little each morning. He wasn't hard to ride, unless I was tryin' to roll a smoke, when the horse would buck me, the papers and tobacco off.

"You want me to tie your feet?" Asked Al.

"No," I answered, "after what you just told me, maybe we ought to call off the bet. I don't want to show you how bad a bronc rider I am!"

"OK," says Al, "but next time you want to show me what kind of a bronc rider you are, ask me to tie your feet together some time, around sundown. I'll look you up in the mornin' and see what kind of shape you're in."

"No thanks, Al," I said as I was gettin' up on my horse an' he bucked me off. "I don't think I'll be sayin' anything about my bronc ridin' for awhile," I says, as I was brushin' corral dust off my fanny.

Horse Tradin'

I sorta like to listen to talk an' stories that float around when a bunch of old timers get together. Sometimes the old fellers get a little wound up an' find it hard to stay on their seats. Most of them was pretty good bronc riders in their day an' showed the signs of long hours in the saddle in all kinds of weather, year in and year out.

I was up in Idaho a while back, havin' a cup of coffee in the local cafe. There was a few old timers there recallin' better days. The talk ran through ropin' an' ridin' broncs to mustangin'. The story I remember the best was one about a feller ropin' a mustang.

"You guys take all the credit about ridin' rough horses," says one old timer, "but let me tell you bout a feller who took a mighty rough ride one day an' he wasn't even horseback, but he ended up with a horse gentle broke!"

"He probably stole the horse somewheres," says a bystander.

"Well, he did do a little horse tradin' along the way. This feller, his name was Bob, was a top hand in this area an' this was durin' the days when there was mustangs all over these hills."

"On this particular day," the old timer continued, "We run into a bunch of mustangs an' before I knew it everybody was ridin' 'hell bent for leather' after them horses. This was a good bunch of horses, there wasn't a mare or colt in the bunch. They was young studs that had been run off by the older studs when they come to close to the mares. If a feller could catch one of these horses he might have a good horse one day."

"That day I didn't catch one of them horses, but I did help a feller in with the horse he caught. We was the first riders back to camp an' was just havin' our second cup of coffee when the other riders started driftin' back into camp. Only a couple of them had caught mustangs."

"Most everybody had got back but Bob, Hal an' Will was still out. Bob's horse come in with the reins draggin' but minus the saddle! Some of the fellers started out to look for Bob, but he showed up, ridin' a gentle broke paint horse that I recognized as belongin' to Hal. Bob's shirt was pretty well tore up an' he was bruised up some, but he wasn't hurt none although he looked mighty rough."

"Now in them days, you just didn't go runnin' up to somebody askin' for details. Everybody acted natural, like nothin' had happened figurin' Bob would tell when he felt like it. An even though Bob was grinnin' some when he turned Hal's horse loose, this still wasn't no invitation for questions."

"I did ask Bob, though, if he'd seen anything of Hal an' Will. He said he had, an' 'they'd caught a mustang an' would probably be in before supper.' That's all he said as he went to get him a cup of coffee an' a clean shirt."

"It wasn't long before Hal an' Will come in. Will was ridin' his horse, leadin' a mustang an' Hal was walkin' along behind, proddin' the mustang when needed, although they had him pretty well broke to lead by this time. Hal looked almost as rough as Bob. Some of the fellers thought there may have been some question as to who actually caught the horse."

"I was mighty curious as to what had happened an' didn't have to wait long. Hal was usually mighty talkative an' I figgured him to be ready to talk when everyone was gathered around.

"After supper, when everyone was settlin' back to relax, Will started to prod Hal into tellin' what happened by sayin', 'Why don't you tell these fellers what happened an' how come you was helpin' me break Bob's horse to lead? You can see they's bustin' all over with curiosity."

"'Well,' says Hal, 'That Bob sure has a strange sense of humor. I was right mad at first, but come to think of it, it might make a pretty good story at that. You remember how Will an' me took off after that paint stud? Well, that horse just plum out run us, so we decided to help Bob. We'd seen him chasin' a horse up that box canyon just south of where we was runnin' the paint. We got to the top of the ridge just in time to see Bob's loop settlin' over the head of that mustang. Will an' me decided to set up on the ridge an' watch the show as Bob had most everything under control—that is until his cinch broke.'"

"'Now I'll tell you, when that cinch broke an' that saddle come off, Bob stayed in it. That saddle wasn't on a horse, but Bob was still gettin' a mighty rough ride. Will an' me was goin' to go down an' give Bob a hand, but the mustang stopped. The horse had choked down some an' had stopped for air. Bob started workin' up the rope, hand over hand, but the mustang had got some air an' started to run again. As the saddle comes rollin' by Bob, he jumps on an' takes another ride. The mustang is wantin' some air an' stops again. Bob starts workin' up the rope, but the horse starts again. This is gettin' to be a might interestin' show an Will an' me is startin' to bettin' on Bob an' Will was bettin' on the horse, but we finally decided it was a draw an' started down to help Bob.'"

"'It took us quite a while to get to where Bob was an' I figgured he'd be mighty happy to see us when we got there. Bob didn't say nothin' as we rode up an' Will dropped a loop over the mustang's neck. I got off my horse to see if Bob was OK an' he said he was an' asked me how I liked the show. I started to say I liked it fine, but Bob went to my horse, climbed aboard, waved an' left. I figgured it was all right if he rode my horse back, I'd ride his. Then I realized his horse wasn't around an' I'd either have to ride this mustang back in or walk. I figgured out that the stunt Bob pulled on me an' it made me a little mad to start with an' I didn't do nothin' but get madder when it come to me that I couldn't ride this horse. Even with Will helpin' me get that saddle screwed on, I couldn't ride that horse. I lost track of the times he throwed me off, an' you seen the final result, me helpin' Will break the horse to lead.'"

The old timer who was tellin' this story continued, "Hal had said all he wanted to an' didn't say anythin' else till Bob says to him, 'You can have that horse if you want him, Hal.'

'No,' says Hal, 'I don't want him. I tried to ride him home an' couldn't do it. You can have him Bob, you rode that saddle when it wasn't on him an' if you can do it ridin' him, you deserve him.'"

The old timer was about done with his story, but somebody asked him, "What happened?"

"Well," says the old timer, "Bob took the horse an' he later told me that was the most ignorant an' hardest horse to ride he'd ever rode. But every time Hal was close to here, Bob was sayin' something bout takin' that gentle 'ole mustang home for his dear little ole mother to ride."

The Sleeper

I hired on a pretty big cow outfit in Eastern Utah a few years ago. The wage wasn't to bad but I had to furnish my own horses. I was paid extra money for using my own horses, but not hardly enough to keep them in shoes in that rough, rocky country.

I knew most of the fellers I was riding with although I hadn't rode with them before. The feller I was riding for, Almie, was in charge of three different ranges with a couple of hundred cows on each range. The ranges were located about 90 miles apart, so we spent quite a bit of time trailering our horses between each range to check the condition of the cows, water holes and grass.

When cattle had to be moved, Almie would drop me and the other hands off in the lower country and meet us farther up the country. I was beginning to think Almie was quite a hand.

He'd generally met us with a small bunch of cows an' I assumed Almie was really having to ride to get these cattle.

As the summer wore on an' we had the cattle pretty well where we wanted them, Almie started laying off some of the other hands or having them help on the farm with the irrigating and haying. He'd asked me to keep riding an' he figgured we could pretty well handle it.

On two different occasions Almie ended up on foot. He'd get up, catch his horse an' cuss out the poor critter for falling asleep on the job, get on an' go back to work. After a while, I wondered if his horse falling asleep on the job wasn't a habit or a disease the horse had caught from his rider.

When the rest of the other hands had been dismissed in one way or the other, the system was the same. Almie would drop me off where the work started and I'd meet him farther up the country.

More an more often, when I'd meet him, he'd be in a clump of trees in the shade takin' a nap. The first time or two I'd meet him, I was really concerned, 'cause I'd see the horse first an' think he got bucked off an' was laying hurt somewhere. After a while, I come to expect to find him takin' a nap. This explained why he could use one horse most of the summer and the horse stayed in good shape. I was riding my horses every day an' they was showing the signs of hard work an' not getting an hour or two worth of nap time every day.

There wasn't much I could do about the situation an' I guess he'd been doing this sort of thing all along. But one day, I did disrupt his nap some an' had a lot of fun doing it.

A water trough had developed a leak. To repair it, we'd need some concrete. This water trough was located in a highly inaccessible spot, in the middle of a canyon so steep there was hardly enough room for a horse to turn around. The walls of this canyon was so steep that the tree trunks grew out horizontally a foot or two before turning skyward.

We used a pack horse to carry in the cement, poured it into the trough then Almie sat down on one of those trees an' took a nap. Waiting to see if the mended leak would hold.

I got me a tree about three feet from Almie an had a smoke. There was some cows coming into water, an' they had to pass within six inches of where my foot was hanging. Each time a cow would pass my foot, she'd stop to investigate, then go on.

Almie was sound asleep, snoring. I was about to drop off to sleep when I noticed a bull following some cows down the trail. I was wondering if he would stop to investigate my foot like the cows did.

I'd held still and the bull stopped at my foot just like the cows. He took a little longer investigating than the cows did and I wondered what would happen if I moved my foot suddenly. Almie was still asleep.

I moved my foot real fast, touching the bull on the end of his nose. He was totally unprepared. He blowed, snorted, an' jumped about fifteen feet down the trail, startling the cows at the water trough! I'd started a stamped by moving my foot an' managed to startle Almie.

When he heard the commotion he jumped straight up out of that tree, an' landed on his feet. He was wondering what happened an' I told him I really wasn't sure, but I thought the bull scared the cows.

The bull done more than that, he scared Almie's horse an' the horse run off. Almie had to ride the pack horse back to the truck where his saddle horse was waiting.

This little episode didn't cure Almie of his taking a nap every day, but I did notice that he chose a spot a little farther away from the water trough when he showed up at that water hole at nap time!

Cedar Bark And Road Apples

We had just finished brandin' the tail end of the year's calf crop. We'd turned the cows and calves loose just inside the forest service boundary fence, and was takin' our time gettin' back to the ranch. I'd put a case of beer in a waterin' trough to keep it cool and we kinda picked up the speed as we neared the ranch. The closer we got the faster we went until we were about a hundred yards away when we had a horse race to the water trough with the beer in it.

I don't know who won the horse race, but Dick ended up in the water trough, soakin' wet, passin' out beer. That cold beer was mighty good an' another would have been better, but we turned our horses loose, milked the cow an' fed what stock we had at the home ranch.

After a little supper, Dick an' I went out to the milk cow's pasture, lit a fire an' had another beer. It wasn't long before Paul joined us.

This was a yearly meeting where we sat back an' made plans to attack the hay. Our cowboyin' was about over till fall an' most of the time during the summer would be spent irrigatin' and cuttin' hay. Nobody much liked the hay work but it is one of the necessary evils connected with the cattle business.

The beer was flowin' free an' Dick asked for a cedar bark cigar. Normally, nobody smoked but things got kinda loose after brandin' an' before hayin'. There wasn't any cedar bark handy so I went over to a post pile an' gathered some an' picked up some paper.

When I returned to the fire, I had a big grocery sack in one hand an' a couple of pounds of cedar bark in the other. I sat down at the fire right next to some road apples. These road apples was old an' had been there for some time an' was all dried out. As I put the cedar bark in the paper, I picked up a road apple an' crushed it into the cedar bark. I double wrapped the mixture, held it up for Dick to lick an' give him a light from the fire.

Dick got to puffin' on his cigar an' sippin' on his beer an' he got to feelin' pretty loose. As the evening wore on an' the cigar got shorter, Dick got to slurrin' his words an' spillin' his beer. He did mention though that this was the finest tastin' cigar he'd ever had. I told him it must be the fresh bark I'd used in fixin' it.

We finally hit the sack an' things moved a little slow the next day. Nobody was feelin' their usual self, but Dick was probably draggin' the most. 'Course nobody told him he'd smoked a road apple the night before.

What are road apples? They used to be more common, but can only be found in certain areas now. Road apples are horse manure!

A Cowboy Called Little Bo Peep

Ropin is one of my favorite pastimes, but to often it turns out to be work, for me anyways. As much work as it usually becomes, I still rope every chance I get.

I had a job one summer, when I was goin' to school, on a sheep ranch. The first part of the summer we spent dockin' lambs an the rest of the summer we spent looking for lost sheep. I was startin' to feel like little Bo Peep. I was spendin' lots of time in the saddle, ridin' through hot desert country, followin' tracks but not findin' any sheep. I spent a lot of time ropin' sagebrush an' rocks.

Then one day I found an old ewe an' a couple of lambs shaded up by a waterhole. I had a partner ridin' with me that day, an I hollered over to him that I'd found some sheep an' he'd better hurry if he wanted to rope one. There wasn't no corrals handy.

I got my rope down an' latched onto one of the lambs as he run out from the brush. I had a couple of piggin' strings on my saddle an tied this lamb to a sagebrush. I'd only tied one leg, he could move around some, but he couldn't move around much.

My partner had latched onto the ewe an' the other lamb was nowhere to be seen. I'd hoped he could have caught the other lamb, sometimes when young stock, be they calves, colts or lambs, are spooked, they might run for miles an' be harder than all-get-out to find.

We rode for a hour or so in the general direction the lamb was last seen headed for but couldn't see him or even cut a track on that hard rocky ground.

Knowing that young stock usually returned to the last place it suckled it's mother, we went back to the waterhole, hoping that the lamb had got his last hot meal there. We checked the ewe and lamb that we had caught, an' decided to put the ewe on one side an' the lamb on the other side of the waterhole. By doin' this, we hoped the bleatin' back an' forth between 'em might call the other lamb back, or even call in some others.

All we could do now was wait. As I loosened the cinches on my saddle, I got to thinking that maybe this sheep headin' wasn't a bad job after all. Right now I was thinkin' of layin' down under a sagebrush an' takin' a nap. Nope, this sheepheadin' wasn't to bad, there was two of us, we had two sheep an' they was tied up, our horses was hobble, there just wasn't anything else that needed to be done, except to take a nap an' wait.

It seemed like I'd only closed my eyes when I was awake again. I checked the horses, they was grazin' on what they could find about 30 yards away. I thought I'd have me a smoke when I decided somethin' was wrong. The sheep weren't bleatin'. I checked the sun an' figgured I'd had a nap for right close to two hours. My partner was still asleep.

Then it occurred to me to check the sheep. Everything was OK over by the ewe. She was givin' dinner to her lamb. Subconsciously, I checked the spot where the lamb had been tied. Everythin' over there was OK. The lamb was still tied up, tryin' to find some shade under that sagebrush.

I lit my smoke, an' laid back about half ways, propped up against a rock. It was a might pretty scene, the red sandstone hills an cliffs, gray sagebrush with just enough cedar trees to break the monotony. The waterhole, even though it was man made, fit right in an' added enough contrast to make it right nice. The waterhole was fed by a spring about 70 or 80 yards away an' even though it was a man-made ditch that transported the water, the little bit of grass that growed along its banks was terrific. There wasn't much, couldn't hardly feed a hungry horse, but there was enough to make the sight just perfect.

Yet somethin' was wrong. I couldn't quite put my finger on it, but somethin' just wasn't right. Then it come to me. Before I took my nap, we'd tied up two sheep, but there was three here now.

"The lost sheep has returned to the fold," I whispered as I woke up my partner. He got up an we caught our horses, bridled 'em an' took off the hobbles an' set out to catch the lost lamb, but gettin' a rope on that lamb proved to be harder than we'd originally anticipated. If we could have had a sheep hook with us, we could have saved us a lot of trouble, our horses a lot of wear an' tear an' I'm sure the lamb would have felt a lot better about it too.

Needless to say, we couldn't catch that forty pound lamb, an' pretty soon he got wise to the ways of the rope. There didn't seem to be any way we could convince that lamb to put his head or neck or a leg through that loop.

Now I don't know if it was sheer desperation or if the lamb just wanted to cool off some before he made his getaway, but he headed straight for the middle of that water hole, an' he didn't slow down none 'till he reached it. When he seen us comin' around to the other side where we figgured on catchin' him, he changed his direction. We had a real problem now.

The longer the lamb stayed in the water, the more water his wool soaked up an' the heavier he got. We wasn't really worried about him dryin' up the waterhole, but now it was questionable if we could get him out before he drowned.

Even though he was swimmin' we still couldn't get a rope on him. We'd toss 'em out, but he'd duck under the water, our loops would be floatin' on top an' the lamb would come up a foot or two from our loops. I swear he'd been taught to swim by Tarzan.

We couldn't rope him, an' the longer he stayed in the water the heavier he got. It became clear, to my partner at least, that we couldn't rope him. So he went after the lamb, boots, spurs, chaps an' all. Just as the lamb was going down for the third time, my partner got a hold of him.

He had a rough time bringin' that lamb in, but he had quite a surprise when he got to shore. Soon as he stepped out on dry ground, I flipped a loop over him an' the lamb both. I'd made up my mind to rope that lamb sooner or later. An' it didn't much matter to me that my partner caught him bare-handed first an still had a hold on him.

We took all three sheep home without further incident, but the fellers still laugh when I tell about the time I brought home three woolies an' a lot better smelling sheepheader. I'm mighty careful to tell 'em I roped two of the sheep by myself an' one of 'em while my partner was takin' a bath.

Hayride

My wife approached me with a starry-eyed look in her eyes and a curious smile on her lips.

"What's up?" I was almost afraid to ask. I had seen that look before and I was sure she wanted something. Money is a little short around here and I wasn't sure I could get her what she wanted.

"Spring has finally arrived," she said. "The days are getting warm and the nights aren't bad either. It didn't even freeze last night."

"Yep," I said. Warily.

"It won't be long before you can turn the cows out and relax a little."

"Well, not really. We've got ground to prepare, I'm gonna have to start irrigating, we've got to get some of this machinery fixed up, haul some salt, scatter bulls. There's plenty to be done around here."

"I thought that maybe we could spend some more time together. You've been away a lot, calving your cows and going to bull sales in addition to your regular chores."

I was almost ready to believe that she was ready to concede that I actually did something around here. All winter long as I tracked mud into the kitchen and scattered hay from the front room to the bedroom, she seemed of the opinion that my sole purpose in life was to create work for her and look at cows. Now, perhaps she was finally going to recognize my full worth and give me some credit.

"What did you have in mind, dear?" I was still wary. "Last year I took you to play golf, but I don't think you enjoyed it very much."

"I didn't enjoy it very much," she said. "You made a fool of yourself discussing fertilizers with the golf pro. And he made it very clear, several times in fact, that he was not interested in using your cows to keep the rough trimmed or in cutting and baling it so you could feed your cows!"

"He didn't have no sense!"

"Any sense," she corrected.

"Well at least we agree on that."

"What I had in mind," she continued, ignoring my last few comments, "was that perhaps we could do something alone, just you and me?"

She had my interest now! "What do you want to do, go to a movie, out to eat or go dancing or all three?"

"No!" She was very emphatic. "No, I was thinking of something more romantic."

"What could be more romantic than dinner, a movie and dancing?" I asked.

"A hayride!"

"A hayride? Good Lord honey! I been loading hay an' pitchin' it off to these cows every day all winter long an' I ain't found nothin' romantic about it yet!"

"But we weren't together."

"That's not my fault," I countered. "I've invited you many times."

"To drive or pitch the hay?"

"Either one. You know I'm not fussy."

"Working is not what I had in mind," she curtly replied.

"Well, honey," I said as I threw on the last bale. I had the wagon loaded and was ready to feed. "Its a pretty day today and I've got to feed this load of hay, say that does rhyme. I guess its sorta romantic at that. Get on, you don't want to miss this grand opportunity to go for a hayride with a poetic cow feeder, do you?"

She turned on her heel, muttering something distasteful about cow feeders, farmers, cowboys, cowmen and all men in general.

Very reluctantly, I pitched the hay to the cows, not knowing if I had won, lost or even bettered my position.

Can ATV's Replace The Horse?

It was a cold day to start with an' I didn't relish the idea of following a herd of cows off the mountain. A trace of snow had appeared on the valley floor during the night an' I knew there would be more on top of the mountain.

I'd made arrangements for Bud to pick me up along with my horse an' I'd help him bring his cows home. It was ten o'clock in the morning an' he hadn't showed. I was beginning to feel a little relieved, it was almost to late to head the cattle home an' maybe to late to even start up. Perhaps tomorrow would be a better day. But, Bud called.

'No, it wasn't to late to move the cattle. They should all be by the gate ready to come home, they knew where they were going an' they should be fairly easy to hande. After all, we just had to bring them down the road, about twelve miles, an' corral them on Brush Creek.' It sounded pretty simple over the phone when Bud called, an' I hoped it would be just as easy as I saddled my horse.

It was cold an' I knew it would be colder on the mountain. I don't like cold weather especially having to work in it. An' riding a horse in cold weather is the coldest job there is.

Bud showed up with two teenage boys, two three wheeler motorcycles an' a few bales of hay. We loaded my horse in the trailer with the ATV's an' set out for the mountain.

At eleven o'clock, we had to chain up the truck. While Bud an' I handled that chore, the boys unloaded the ATV's. We were on snow an' ice, but the boys figured if they had to work, they might just as well have fun while they did it. An' they did have fun. We lost sight of them shortly after we got going again. But, judging from their tracks an' skid marks, they must have had quite a time.

It was noon when we reached the holding pasture where Bud had been keeping the cattle. Just like Bud had said, the cattle were waiting at the gate, ready to come home. On the way up, we passed a few truck-loads of calves coming down. Somebody had weaned their calves today an' I remember thinking that it was a bad day to wean an' truck calves back to the ranch. I also figured we were lucky. Bud had weaned his calves two weeks before so we had a herd of mostly cows with ten or fifteen yearling steers to contend with. It might be easy going, if we could get going.

Bud opened the gate an' counted out the cows. "We're short 14 head," he said. "I guess we better look for them while we're here."

The boys went ahead on the ATV's while Bud an' I checked as many areas as we could from the truck. Bud's horse was still in the corral at his camp an' I didn't really want to leave the warmth of the truck. But when the boys reported back an' indicated that they had only found seven of the missing cows an' they were scattered, I knew the warmth of the truck would soon be lost.

An hour of riding had all fourteen of the missing cows found. Bud sent one of the boys on his three-wheeler ahead to check the main part of the herd an' the other boy an' myself followed the newly found cows. When we got to the road, Bud went ahead.

Following the cows, I took note of the ATV an' it's rider. He was warmer than I, fancy gloves, a face mask an' a snow suit. My chaps an' heavy winter coat did help, but he looked warmer. I wondered if he had a heater, blowing nice warm air out from under the cowling onto his feet to help him.

Later, I decided the ATV wasn't much help. I'd seen the TV commercials on them things an' they looked real nice, but this was a little rougher country with the rocks, sagebrush, hills, a few trees an' snow. It didn't look like the boy with me was having as smooth a ride as I was.

I noticed also that everywhere my companion went on his three-wheeler, he went at full speed an' the sound of his machine made a lot of noise. Enough noise in fact to scare the cows off the trail. I finally hollered at the kid an' made him follow along behind the cattle at a much slower speed. He didn't like it much, but to me this was work an' the sooner we got it done, the sooner we could get warm.

We got to Bud's camp an' I had a surprise. Bud wasn't there, neither was the boy, an' there were some cattle that didn't belong here.

I started sorting Bud's cattle an' sending them down the road to the west. I let the stray cattle be. There was a fork in the road here an' it was fairly easy to keep the strays. But it was rough trying to sort the cattle on the ice. My horse got to watching the cattle closer than his footing an' slipped a couple of times, going down to his knees both times. But he recovered an' we got the job done. The ATV wasn't any help an' the boy spent most of the time in Bud's camp.

Soon however, I noticed more of Bud's cows coming from the east. An' it wasn't long before Bud an' the boy showed up. A short conference revealed what happened.

The cows had come to the forks in the road before the boy had got there. They were supposed to go west, but half went east an' the other half went west. The neighbor who had weaned his calves earlier in the day, well, his cows broke out an' had got mixed with Bud's.

I'd lost track of time, but the sun was fast getting ready to set. We had no idea of how many of the neighbor's cows we had or how many of Bud's cows we had or where they were. Some could even be past the corrals on Brush Creek.

There were two sets of corrals between where we were an' Brush Creek. They were only wire corrals, but we figured we had better get what we had corralled an' look for what might be missing later. If we hadn't taken the time to look for the fourteen missing cows earlier we might have saved ourselves a lot of problems. But we had cattle out an' we were committed. It was going to be a long day.

The main part of the herd was just approaching the rim of the mountain as the sun went down. We sent one of the boys ahead to turn the cows into the wire corrals. Once we got the leaders turned an' baited the inside of the corral with some hay, it was just a matter of hurrying up the stragglers an' closing the gate.

When that was done, it was after dark, fog was rolling in an' occasionally the moon an' stars could be seen through the fog. We loaded my horse into the trailer to go down the mountain an' see if we could find any cows that had got a head start. The boys thought it would be more fun if they rode their three-wheelers ahead of us.

The cab of that pickup was mighty warm an' mighty welcome. Bud had saddled his horse, but had only spent an hour or so horseback. I'd been out since we looked for an' found the missing cattle. I knew it was impossible, but I found myself hoping we wouldn't find anymore of Bud's cattle that had got past us. We did, but Bud said I'd got cold enough an' we'd let the boys on the ATV's get ahead of them an' open the gate to the second wire corral.

That proved to be a mistake. The boys, figuring that the hardest part of the days work was over, got to fooling around on their three-wheelers an' had a wreck.

Bud an' I didn't know it, we were in the truck trying to hurry the stragglers. But one of the boys came back to report the accident. The other boy was hurt, but not serious, was the report. Shortly after he arrived, he ran out of gas in his ATV.

It was back into the cold for me. I had to follow the stragglers while Bud went ahead to check on the wreck an' turn the cattle. The fog had raised, it was clear an' cold an' the wind had started up. It took another hour or so to get the stragglers corralled, an' I ended up walking the last couple of hundred yards or so. My feet had got cold an' I decided to walk an' see if I couldn't get them warmed up some.

The wreck on the ATV wasn't to serious although it did put one of the machines out of commission, an' we decided after we corralled our horses an' threw them a bale of hay, that we'd better have the one kid checked out in the emergency room of the hospital. It was after eleven o'clock according to the truck radio when we headed toward town.

I got to thinking that I had put in a twelve hour day for Bud an' most of it out in the cold on horseback. I got to thinking also about what we had accomplished. We had started out with most of the cattle we wanted, found all the missing cattle an' should have a good day. But our herd got split when half went the wrong way, we got them mixed when the neighbor's cattle broke out an' we didn't know how many cattle we had or whose. What cattle we did have, we had in two different corrals neither one of which was the one we had intended to use. We were also sure that we had some cows somewhere that we didn't know.

We had also started late, by three or four hours according to the way I like to work stock. We'd also had a wreck with the ATV's which put one out of commission an' injured one boy.

I came to the conclusion that the ATV's might be alright for checking fence or changing pipe or other ranch jobs, but I didn't want them around when I was working cattle, for a number of reasons, namely, too much noise, to much speed an' not the right kind of control on stops an' turn backs that's needed when working cattle. Besides that, a wreck had put one machine out of commission. My horse had fell a couple of times but we still had to suffer through the cold an' get the work done. One of the machines had run out of gas, but my horse hadn't an' I came to the conclusion that the ATV's weren't of much use that day.

But if those machines had a heater, maybe...

Where's All The Cows?

It was a working holiday. We had decided to mix business with pleasure by gathering some cattle, branding a few late calves and doctoring a few lame cows. We'd take the horses, wives and kids, not necessarily in that order and have a picnic and a branding at the same time.

So here we were, two truckloads of horses, two pickup loads of wives and kids, stopped at the last general store on the way to the mountain, loading up with extra hot dogs, soda pop and picnic supplies.

A woman loaded down with the same sort of groceries stopped us on her way out. "I couldn't help but notice all your horses," she said, "But wheres all the cows?" She pointed towards two cars with trailers and Florida licence plates.

"We've been all over the country on our vacation," she continued, "And we haven't really seen any cows or cowboys."

"We're sure enough cowboys," chipped Dave. "Our horses are in the truck an' we're goin' where the cows are."

"We'd sure like to see some cows, just like the old west on our vacation," she said.

"Well," said Dave, "just follow us. We're goin' to have some real old west fun today."

"Fun", I thought. "This so called fun turns into work real fast."

We got our supplies and our caravan of trucks headed up the mountain, joined by two touring cars from Florida. On the way up, I started to cuss Dave.

"There wasn't no need to go invitin' all them people up here with us," I said. "Why, with our wives an' all our kids, we already got an overstocked dude ranch on our hands."

"They won't hurt nothin'," said Dave. "Besides, they just want to watch some cowboys."

"They could have went to a rodeo, they're plenty of them around."

"You sure you're not worried about your horse buckin' you off in front of all them folks? Or do you think your ropin' could use some polishin' up before you rope in front of a crowd?"

"Dave, I thought I gave up the dude business years ago."

"Don't tell me you forgot all your tailor-made, ready to use excuses!"

"I never needed 'em," I countered.

"Just humor these folks for a day. It might turn out to be sorta fun."

We got to where the corrals were and unloaded the horses, in the middle of a crowd of people. We didn't have any extra horses, but did manage to double up some of the kids and Dave volunteered his horse to the woman we'd met in the general store. I was riding a colt that I'd started sometime ago, and declined to take any extra riders.

I'd brought this colt along specifically so as I could start roping off him. I'd put plenty of miles on him and figured it was time to start further-ing his education, even though he still blowed up every so often. In fact, he really took to me when I stepped on him, and some of the visitors felt somewhat relieved that I hadn't volunteered my horse like Dave did.

I really didn't see how they could enjoy this. Dave and I had gathered the cattle, about 300 head of mother cows and their calves, and put them in a small holding pasture. It was all work to me, long hours in the saddle, and today would just be a different kind of work.

The cattle weren't all that hard to gather, and I found myself herding a few of our "guests" into the corrals along with the cows.

Dave had stayed behind and built a fire and got the branding irons hot. I took down my rope and started to catch a few calves. The first calf I caught, much to my surprise, and I was surprised even more when I heard a light round of applause coming from our visitors. The big surprise came when I turned my horse towards the fire and he started bucking. He didn't buck to hard, but we did manage to scatter everyone around the fire.

I got the horse settled down and Dave branded the calf. He also an-swered a lot of questions about branding and the need for it.

We only had twenty or so calves to brand and I did all the roping. I volunteered my horse to the other adults, but after he'd bucked twice that day, nobody offered to rope. As I drug the calves in, I looked for cows that needed some doctoring. There weren't to many and I got to thinking that with a little luck, we might get done early and have part of the day to sit back and enjoy a picnic.

It didn't take long to finish up on the calves, then Dave and I roped a few cattle that needed a shot. By the time we finished, the smaller kids had started roasting hot dogs over the fire.

The adults ate after we turned the cows out. Over dinner, the conversation centered mostly on the west, cattle, horses and ranch life in general. I was surprised when our visitors thanked me for providing a day of action for them. I figured it just came with the job.

The lady from Florida kept remarking how quiet and peaceful it was. She couldn't get over the view and I had to admit it was nice, and it was peaceful.

I remarked, "When I camp up here, I generally put up a tent right under that tree, and I've had more than one cup of coffee watchin' the sun come up an' the deer come into water. It is sorta nice."

"Lovely, lovely," commented the lady. "Certainly much, much better than what we can look at in Florida."

"What do you see in Florida?" In my mind, I had already answered my question, envisioning miles of beaches, a lot of bikinis and a lot of pretty girls filling those bikinis.

"Alligators!"

"What?"

"Alligators," replied the woman from Florida. Every morning when we wake up, there is an alligator or two in our back yard. I would much rather wake up and watch deer, like you do."

"What do you do with an alligator in your back yard?"

"Nothing, there's not really much you can do with an alligator."

"Well," I said " that's my style, nothing."

I got up to unsaddle my horse. "You know," I said, "It's very hard to imagine an alligator in a bikini."

The Bull Rider

A big, reddish-brown hulk settled into a chute. The animal, a bull, was calm in his movements and seemed almost dignified.

A tall, slim, muscular cowboy watched the bull. Outwardly, he appeared calm. But inside he was tense. His stomach was in knots. His muscles were tense, trained to respond instantly to his every command. He was a little nervous and he had a right to be; he was going to try to ride that bull; he was a bull rider.

"This one might be my number," he thought as he climbed the chute. He had a number of alternatives. He could ride and win or he could ride and lose. Worse, he could be bucked off and injured, perhaps even killed.

"Right or left handed?"

"Right," he answered as he dropped a plaited rope down the side of the bull. He sat down on the bull, put his right hand in the braided hand hold and slid the rope into the right position. Although he was paying very careful attention to what he was doing, he had some recurring thoughts about the possible outcome of this meeting.

He had secondary visions of being hurt when this was over, being hurt and lifted into the back end of an ambulance for a fast ride to the hospital. He's seen it before.

"Not a bad set of horns," he thought as he studied the bull's head. The bull had his head turned, partly watching the going on. The bull was calm, but there was a proud look in his eyes, a proud spirit which seemed to say "look out". Or was it a murderous look, intent on adding another victim to perhaps a long list of others?

There they were, an object, a living object, to be conquered and the one who proposed to conquer, studying each other.

"How's that?"

"Pull it up just a little tighter," answered the cowboy. He was having a battle with himself, and he was used to it. He went through it every time he got on a bull.

"That's tight enough, let's wrap it up." With his hand in the hand hold, he took the end of the rope, laid it across his palm, back under his fingers and across his palm again. This was all he had to hold on to. He would try to stay on that bull by the grip in his hands, the muscles in his legs and his balance.

He was ready now. For the first time, he looked into the arena and out into the crowd. He took a long look at he clowns. His own welfare could lie in their hands.

"The next rider, out of chute number four on the bull..." The announcer's voice was shut out of the cowboy's mind. Now it was his turn, what would happen when the chute gates opened? Could he ride good enough to make money? Would he be cheered for making a good ride or would he be mourned for by his wife, family and friends? Would he walk away form this bull, or would he be carried away? What?

"This bull will probably cut back to the right on the second jump and start a spin." The cowboy who helped tighten the rope was telling him this.

"Cut back right and spin. Okay." Now, he thought to himself, get those legs set right, twist that arm around in the right position. Keep your toes out.

One last look to see that the judges were ready and the clowns were in the right position. He hadn't heard what the announcer had been saying, he hadn't heard the crowd yelling. All there was in the world was just the bull, himself and a large empty feeling in his stomach that was getting larger every second.

There were a lot of places he would rather have been, but he had to ride that bull out of the chute, he had to try to win the prize money. This was how he made his living, and he must try, regardless of the circumstances. Something inside him kept fighting down the growing fear.

"This is it," he thought, "maybe I don't have anything to worry about."

"As soon as this critter has his head right, turn him out, boys."

"You ready, son?" One of the chute hands was asking the question as he loosened the latch. All that kept the bull confined was this fellow pressing his weight against the gate.

"Never could get over the fear," he though as he watched the bull's head.

The bull turned his head, he was watching the gate now. The bull was ready.

"Outside!" The cowboy felt the bull tense up as the gate was swinging open. He felt strangely relaxed, but tense at the same time. He was ready for the first jump.

The gate was open.

The Dude

The new hand showed up one afternoon durin' a rainstorm. Nobody seen him come in but he was here, big as life standin' in the doorway with a new hat, new boots an' new everything on. He sorta looked like an actor out of an old cowboy movie, an doin' his best to look bowlegged.

Ron noticed him first, an' seein' the new clothes says, "Sorry fella. We don't take rides out in the rain." That wasn't exactly true. The boss of this outfit was a money grabbin' son - of - a - gun that would send anybody out in a rainstorm, blizzard or hurricane if some dude was willing to pay for it. An' to people in their right minds, it would be mighty surprisin' how many dudes wanted to go ridin' in all kinds of bad weather. 'Course if the dude got sick, he could rest an' recuperate a couple of days. But us dude wranglers couldn't get a day off for anything short of death.

"Well," says the feller, "I was lookin' for the foreman. I'm supposed to start work for him today."

"He's down at the night corrals, 'bout a mile an' a half down the road."

The dude said "thanks" an' started down the road, packing a suitcase an' walkin'. Ron watched him walkin' down the road an' remarked to the rest of us that he was tryin' to walk like he'd been in the saddle "all his life."

"Yep," says Pete. "The boss will see that walk, tell him we don't hire cripples, an' he'll straighten right up like an old range mare that's just had her feet trimmed. Especially if he wants the job."

I guess that's about what happened, 'cause when he bedded down in the bunkhouse that night he didn't seem to have as much trouble gettin' around as he'd had earlier in the day.

It was plain to see the new hand didn't know much about horses or their equipment when we was saddling up the next mornin' 'cause he didn't seem to do much but get in the way. 'Bout all he could do was mess things up.

When it come time to jingle the horses up to the corrals where we would rent out rides for the day, the new feller looked like he'd put in a half-a-days work an' it was only 'bout a hour an a half since the sun had come up. The boss showed him a good, gentle dude horse to ride an' we started to drive the horses to the day corrals.

The dude business is normally pretty slow with nothin' more than a couple of dudes fallin' off their horses for excitement so when we drove the horses up to the day corrals we done it real western, on the run with a lot of hoopin' an' hollerin' an the like. Somewheres along the way the new feller lost control of his horse an' we ended up hazin' him in the corral with the rest of the horses. He was sorta pale when we caught his horse an' helped him off.

He was a dude tryin' to be a cowboy on a dude outfit. I guess he figured it didn't take much to be a cowboy, just ride a horse around some. But he got along real well with the customers so the boss kept him on. It wasn't all uncommon to see him with a bunch of dudes givin' 'em a line of bull. I guess that's the only reason the boss kept him on, to keep the other dudes busy while they was waitin' for their turns.

After a couple of days, when the dude had learned to keep his saddle horse under control when we jingled the other horses up to the day corrals, he was given a colt to ride. On this outfit, every hand had a colt to ride an' as soon as the boss figured the colt could go into the dude string, the hand would be given a new colt an' the cycle would start all over.

We was all interested in what colt the boss would give the dude to ride. Them colts that was a little ranker than others was already bein' rode so there wasn't much that could give the dude a heck of a lot of trouble, but there was a couple of horses that had the promise of making a pretty fair horse. The experienced hands sorta took a little pride in the colts they rode an' turned out an' it meant a fifty dollar bonus to the hand that could turn out the best colt at the end of the season. So, everybody was mighty interested in the colt the dude would get 'cause some of the fellers had been givin' their favorites a little help after hours.

There wasn't a hand on the place that wasn't relieved when the boss give the dude a horse called Mule Ear. The colt had got the name from his ears an' more than one hand had said he wouldn't "be caught dead on a horse that looked like that." Mule Ear not only had long ears, he had a big head an' a peaked rump like a mule. The colt was gentle enough, he'd never even offered to buck the first time he was tried. The horse just didn't look like a horse.

The only problem with Mule Ear was that he'd turn into you when you got on. This ain't a bother, but it can be disastrous in the dude business, like when you're tryin' to get some 250 pound woman on a horse an' the horse moves. I've seen many a cowboy tryin' to balance some of them heavy-weight gals with one hand an' hold onto the horse with the other. The looser usually ends up to be the cowboy, diggin himself out from under the gal who's usually sayin' somethin' like, "I haven't done much riding in the last few years."

But the dude didn't mind this fault of Mule Ear's. It seemed like he'd taken it on himself to cure Mule Ear of this bad habit, an' with the help of a few older hands he'd made some progress after a few weeks.

Sometimes, when the work was slow, the boss would send some of the fellers out to the flat to work their colts. On this particular day, the boss had given me an' the dude some time to work these colts and I was to meet the dude out on the flat. Usually, these times in the flat with the dude were welcome. It meant that a feller could sneak a snooze while the dude rode Mule Ear an' kept a lookout for the boss.

I guess I was sorta lookin' forward to takin' a snooze. The dude had started out an' all I had to do to get my nap was switch saddles from my guide horse to my colt an' I was ready. Saddlin' my colt wasn't much of a job an' I was on my way. I hit a fast lope out the corral gate.

The dude was walkin' Mule Ear around in the pines as I caught up to him. I slowed down some but my colt an' me passed the dude an' Mule Ear. As we went past, I hollered, "Hurry up, we'll be late!"

The next thing I heard was the sound of beating hooves. I turned in the saddle an' seen the dude leavin' Mule Ear somewhat unexpectedly an' rollin up under a pine tree, just like a bowlin' ball. I pulled up my colt.

"You alright, Dude?"

"Yes. Where's my horse? Is he OK?"

"Yep." Mule Ear was standin' where he stopped, reins hangin' on the ground. I rode over an' caught Mule Ear. "Here he is, sound as a dollar."

"I won't say anything," I says. "Just wake me up when the boss shows. I'll be under that tree."

"OK. I'll make a good horse out of this nag yet!"

I was laughin' to myself as I hobbled my colt an' stretched out under a pine tree. "Make a good horse out of him! He's probably got thoughts of pickin' up that $50. on that nag." Thoughts of the dude's statements and determination left me as the season wore on. Soon it was fall an' the dude business was fallin' off as vacationin' families returns home for school. An' it soon come time for us to wrap up operations at the dude outfit.

We'd all been expectin' it, so no one was surprised when the boss calls everybody together an' says, "Some of you guys have worked three of four colts for me an' I sure do appreciate that. We got some good horses here, an' they'll be better next year. But to give everybody a fair chance at this fifty bucks, I want you all to get the best colt you have an' bring him out an show what you've done with him."

Everybody was saddlin' his best colt. Everybody except the dude. He'd only had one colt an everybody figured he was out of the runnin' with Mule Ear. But he was saddlin' him up.

There was a fine horse show that afternoon. A lot of good hands was showin' what they could do an' they'd done a lot with their colts. There was some mighty good reinin' horses put to the test that day. Rollbacks, spins, slidin' stops, the colts done everything. Then come the dude's turn.

Slowly, he led Mule Ear to the center of the corral. He'd seen some good horses work, figure he was out of the runnin' but he was goin' to try. Somewheres along the line he'd picked up somethin' every good cowboy has, the will to try. He turned Mule Ear around, facin' the boss an' mounted. Slowly, he walked the horse around in a circle, turned him around and walked him up to the boss an' stopped him. It wasn't much of a show compared to what the other fellers had done an' he was gettin' some friendly jerrin' from 'em. Some of the fellers figured they had that fifty bucks sewed up.

The dude was sittin' on Mule Ear in front of where the boss was standin' an' for all practical purposes, he was done. He started to tip his hat to the boss when a gust of wind come up an' blowed his hat to the ground. Mule Ear just stood there an' looked at the hat an' then the dude as he jumped down to get it.

"That's it, I guess," says the dude. He's leadin' Mule Ear out.

"Hold on, son," The boss says. "I'm just about to make the award."

I'm beginnin' to wonder if this fifty buck bonus might be little harder to come by as I look over the rest of the hands. He's mighty careful as he looks into the eyes of each man.

"Fellers," starts the boss, "I've seen some mighty good horsemanship here today, mighty good. An' if I hadn't seen some fo them horses last spring, I'd swear they had been in trainin' longer than this summer. But," the boss was pickin' his words mighty careful, "I'm givin' the bonus money to the dude this year. He earned it!"

There was harsh words among the hands. But a simple, "How come?" seems to raise a question in the bosses' mind.

"How come?"

"Yea," says Ron. "We turned out some mighty good horses for you an' you've givin' this bonus to dude who don't know nothin' 'bout a horse or for that matter, anything!"

"Well," says the boss, "Ron an' for that matter, the rest of you, I'm sure not givin' the bonus to the dude because I like him, 'cause you an' me both know he ain't much as far as a cowboy goes. But he does have the promise of bein' a cowboy someday. He's gettin' the bonus 'cause he took a horse nobody else wanted an' made a good dude horse out of him. You guys took your colts an' made good horses out of them, they'll spin, pivot, whatever you want. But where you guys missed the boat was that a dude horse don't have to do these things. A dude horse just has to be dependable an' reliable. The dude turned out the most dependable horse of all of you. I guess what I'm tryin' to say is that for this business, your colts have been over trained. Not every dude knows that he can turn a horse by a touch of the spur. You guys have turned out colts that any horse trainer in the country might be interested in for a prospect, but the dude has turned out a horse that can be used by any dude in the country if he comes here. See what I mean?"

"I guess so," says one of the hands. "But us fellers put in a lot of time makin' good horses out of them colts. An' we made some pretty good horses out of them. It sure seems like a waste."

"It ain't a waste," says the boss, "There's a fifty dollar bonus for each of you what shows up next season, payable the first day as long as you remember that were lookin' for good horses, horses that anybody can ride. Just remember that I'm lookin' for good dependable horses an' more than likely, not a one of them will ever have to cut out cow. I'm just lookin' for horses that a dude can ride out an' look at the scenery on. That's it."

There was a lot of sorry looks on the faces of the hands as the boss picked up his cane an' hobbled away. But there was a few fellers sayin' that it sure makes it easier on us when we don't have to bring somebody in with a busted leg.

I don't know how the hands felt, but there was a few of them the next season lookin' for fifty dollars an' a job. I don't know what happened to the dude, but heard he'd got a job in public relations somewheres. Don't know but it wasn't for the same company.

Fake

At the last Old Timers Rodeo, where all the competitors had to be over 40, the bull that I drawed, bucked me off rather unceremoniously after a very short ride. I wasn't hurt, an' the bull didn't give me any trouble after we parted company.

"Is this an Old Timers Rodeo?" I yelled up to the announcer.

"Yes, this is an Old Timers Rodeo," he replied.

"Well then, I think it's a fake," I yelled back.

"A fake? What do you mean a fake?"

"Well," I says, "That bull ain't near as old as I am!"

A Lucky Catch?

I really love to rope. But I'm not much good at it. I use what practice time I get to have fun rather than get better. That's probably one of the reasons I'm such a poor roper - everytime I have to shake out a loop to catch something for some doctorin' or whatever, I figured it's another time to get some practice in an' I generally end up havin' a lot of fun an' not catchin' much.

Given enough time I can generally catch a crippled cow or a sick calf to give it a shot or some doctorin'. I'm often accused of just catchin' the stuff that wants to be caught, the stuff that ain't healthy enough to get away. That might be right - I generally feel more comfortable ropin' in an enclosed area, such as a corral or small pasture (the smaller the better) where the stock bein' caught don't have a good chance to get away. But, just because the stock don't have a good chance to get away don't necessarily mean they stand a better chance of bein' caught. But, ropin' cattle is a lot of fun.

Ropin' horses is a little different. Whenever I had to rope a horse, I always got sorta serious, more business like. Horses, for me are harder to catch, although there ain't nothin' easy. An' it always seemed more fun to rope cattle on horseback than to rope horses on foot. But horses always seem to get a little more nervous when they're bein' roped, so a feller really can't get as much practice ropin' them as he can ropin' cattle.

Out on some of the larger outfits in Neveda, Wyoming and Montana, the only way to catch your horse for the days work is with a rope. On some of these places, one man, generally the cowboss or some other highly respected roper, would rope out your horse for you. Not only did he have to know all the horses in the cavy, but he had to be mighty handy with a rope.

On one outfit that I worked for, the jingle boy roped out the horse you called for. He was mighty good with a rope, had perfected all the neat throws, knew every horse in the cavy an' even told the buckaroos what horses in their strings needed shoein' or had went lame. It was a real pleasure to watch him work.

Some outfits made a feller catch his own horse. I was always mighty careful when I worked on these kind of ranches. Sometimes there wasn't much courtesy showed on some of these places, an' if more than one roper was in the corral at one time, a feller could get run over or get someone else run over. Most of the time, only one man caught a horse at a time.

On one of these outfits, I had to rope my own horse one morning. I made such a pretty throw, the loop settled out there just like it was supposed to, an' such a pretty catch, that I was really embarrassed. I had caught the wrong horse! But I didn't want to admit it. So I mumbled something about never seein' this horse rode before an' lead him out of the corral.

R. LOREN
SCHMIDT

Nobody had this horse in their string, so, rather than admit that everything that had worked so well was just a fluke, I decided to ride the horse I
caught. That was a mistake! The horse bucked me off three times before I
finally got him lined out an' it was a fight all day long with him. I do know
I'd have been better off if I had turned him loose that mornin' an' tired
myself out tryin' to rope the horse I had wanted.

On my own place, I liked to have my horse gentle enough so as I
could catch them easy. But I did have one that was hard to catch. I either
had to rope him or get him cornered so as he couldn't hardly move. Havin'
plenty of work to do everytime I needed this horse an' not havin' the time
to play with him, I figured I'd just have to rope him the rest of his life.

I had to catch this horse one day, an' I separated him from the other
horses. I had him in the round corral, but I couldn't corner him there, so I
got the rope out.

After one clean miss he was gettin' pretty nervous, an' I was afraid
he'd try to jump the fence. I figured I had one last chance at him. I made
my loop real careful, took one swing, hoolighan style, of course, an' let the
rope slide off my fingers. It snaked out there real pretty, opened up an'
settled down, just like it was supposed to, except it settled down right over
a fence post!

I'd missed my horse an' roped a post. The horse ducked away at the
last second, but he couldn't turn away fast enough, an' was standin' next to
the fence with the rope tight up against his chest. He was afraid of the rope
an' afraid to move. After that, I never roped that horse, I just tossed the
rope over his withers an' he was caught.

But on that day, I missed him, but I'd caught him. A lucky miss an' a
lucky catch.

Changin' Names

The little gray mare come through the sale one day. She sure looked good, straight legged, slicked up an' not showing any of the rough winter hair the other horses was showing at this time of year. She was put up pretty well an' showed some breedin', good breedin', of the sort that wasn't common among most of the cow horses in the country.

I bid on her when she come through the sale ring, I even bid past what money I had on me. I wanted her pretty bad. But somebody wanted her worse than I, so I quit biddin'. Good thing too, 'cause I'd bid her past what I could even borrow money to pay for her.

I was needin' some extra horses an' I figured this little three year old mare might fit in. I had plenty of ridin' an' the mare was started some. But I didn't get her, an' was real surprised to see her in the horse corrals the next mornin'.

My boss had wanted her pretty bad an' he ended up buyin' her from the feller who bought her at the sale barn. He wouldn't say how much he had to give for her, but I know it was plenty, 'cause I knew when I quit biddin'. I figured she was a mighty expensive little horse.

The boss asked me if I'd ride the horse an' give her some education. After some hagglin' over how much extra I'd see in my paycheck for this little service, we decided I'd take the horse an' I'd have a free hand with her.

What I ended up doin' was takin' the mare home an' let my wife sorta mess with her a few weeks. My wife had expressed an interest in doin' some horse breakin' an' this gray didn't have a mean bone in her body, just a nice little horse. So, I figured this little idea of mine would work out pretty well for both of them, the wife would gain some experience in horse breakin' an' the mare would learn something about people.

Well, this idea worked out pretty good for a week or two. Then I come home one night, just about dark, an' the gray was standin' in the corral, with the saddle on an' no one was in sight. The wife was in the house, nursin' some new bruises. Apparently, the little gray mare had bucked her off, an' she was sore enough she didn't even unsaddle her.

This whole situation sorta made me mad. I was sure there wasn't a buck in the horse - I'd rode her myself. I was certain that the wife had done something to bring this on, an' that sorta ticked me off too!

I still had my spurs on, an' I set out to see if this little gray could really buck. My wife, she sorta hobbled an' limped out to watch me get dusted.

Straightenin' out the wife's saddle a bit, I climbed aboard. Now I did everything I could think of from cussin' an' cajolin' to spittin' an' spurrin' to get her to buck, but she wouldn't. I took my hat an' was wavin' it an' slappin' it from her head, ears an' eyes back to her rump without any success, much to my consternation.

I was still very convinced there wasn't a buck in the mare an' my wife was just as convinced she hadn't done anything to encourage the horse to buck. I decided that if this horse was goin' to be good for me an' buck for the wife, I ought to be ridin' her. Besides, my horses up at the cow camp was gettin' plenty of work an' initiatin' the gray to some cow work would give them an extra day off. Besides that, too, my wife expressed a sudden disinterest in breakin' horses.

I fed the mare in the corral that night. The next day, she got a ride to the cow camp an' that day I pointed her to some cow work. She worked pretty an' even earned a regular turn in the rotation of my string. Each day I rode her, my wife would ask how she was or if anything happened. I was happy to report that the mare was comin' along real nice an' that nothin' really excitin" really happened. I didn't put much stock in her warnings that someday something would happen and I'd better watch myself.

It did happen one day. I just finished fixin' a water trough an' stepped on the mare when she started buckin'. I don't know to this day what set her off, but the first three jumps she took I rode her standin' up, with my left foot in the stirrup an' my right foot just hangin' there.

It occurred to me durin' those free jumps that I had given ridin' lessons to dudes an' told them that "ridin' was simple. You just put your right leg on the right side of the horse an' your left leg on the left side an' keep your mind in the middle!" It also occurred to me that I was not doing just that, an' that part of my anatomy I referred to as my mind was NOT in the middle! While I was figurin' out what to do about this situation, I happened to remember that every time I had deviated from keepin everything where it belonged, I got bucked off!

I managed to get my leg where it belonged an' was still fishin' for the stirrup when I got the mare stopped. I'd lost my hat somewheres an' found it, just by chance in the last place where I would have looked for it, in the bottom of the water trough.

By the time I got back to the cow camp, fed the horses an' headed for home, my hat still hadn't dried out. Both it an' my hair was still wet when I walked into the house. My wife knew it was the day to ride the little gray mare, an' she noticed my wet hat an' hair, but didn't say anything.

I brought up the subject of the gray mare by sayin', "I rode One-Side Surprise today."

"One-Sided Surprise? Which horse is that?"

"That's the little gray mare," I answered.

"Oh," she said. "But isn't that kind of a long name for you to give a horse? You generally name them with one word names like Stupid or Knothead or something like that, then refer to them with shorter names, those four-letter names."

"Well," I says, "If she pulls anymore stunts like she did today I can change her name."

One-Sided Surprise an' me got along pretty well for a while. Then one day I changed her name to "Misguided Thinking". On that day I did not get my mind in the middle!

A Tough Day

I knew it was goin' to be a tough day. I'd went to town to get supplies, stayed in town overnight, an' here it was day break. I'd already had a flat tire on the truck this mornin', an' now I was openin' a gate right next to cattle guard. The reason I was openin' the gate rather than drivin' through was because some fool cow had went an' got herself caught in it.

The way I'd had it figured, by now I'd have been in the saddle, gatherin' cattle to move farther up the mountain. But now, it looked like I'd be three or four hours late even gettin' started what with havin' to get a tire changed, havin' to get this cow out of her predicament, puttin' my supplies away camp, catchin' a horse an' headin' out. I found myself wishin' I could turn around an' go back to town. After all, I'd had a lot better time dancin' with them gals last night than I figured I was goin' to have today.

I got the cow freed from the cattle guard, although she ended up in the wrong pasture from where she should have been. I went on to camp, took care of my housekeeping chores, caught a horse an' got started. Now when I start out to have a miserable day, I do a bang-up job of it.

Right off the bat, I had to rope a cow an' doctor her for pinkeye. She was kinda wild an' when I finally got a rope on her, it took more than one throw, I missed my dallies an' lost my rope. By the time I got my rope back, dallied up an' got the cow doctored, I bet she was thinkin' that the cure was worse than the disease. I know I was havin' some doubts about how much I had helped her.

I got a few cows gathered an' headed in the right direction. I had a few late calves to earmark an' made a loop an' started. Normally, this would have been fun, but today, for some reason or other, it wasn't. It was work.

I got one calf caught an' earmarked without to much trouble, an' caught another one. Soon as that second calf hit the end of the rope, he let out a beller that spooked that herd of cows an' me too! An' he kept it up. I half hitched my rope to the saddle horn an' stepped off to earmark this calf.

He kept bellerin', an' for such a little feller, he sure made a racket. An' he kept it up an' was still bellerin' when I got done. His mom showed up, just as I stood up. Now I don't know what was on her mind, but I could see from the look in her eye that she wasn't pleased with what I'd done to her baby. She must have decided that I was the source of all the trouble an' all the racket, 'cause she took after me.

I couldn't make it to my horse, so I got behind a tree. She chased me around the tree three or four times then tires of it, a little. I was plumb tired. I had my bat wing chaps on, an' my spurs, an' it was difficult to keep ahead of the cow dressed that way. I'd have climbed the tree, but I can't even climb stairs dressed that way. I managed to shed my chaps when the cow stopped for a breather, an' made a dash for my horse.

The horse was real hard to catch with me runnin' at him an' that cow tryin' to catch me, but somehow or another I managed an' got on. The cow was mighty protective of her calf an' I was havin' a problem gettin' my rope off. After what seemed like most of the day, I finally managed to get the rope off the calf. The cow an' calf seemed more than willing to tell them where to go. Luckily, they headed off in the direction they was supposed to an' they wasn't takin' any spare time in goin'.

I got my chaps an' started to make another gather. The cows I'd already got had continued in the right direction an' I could catch up to them later.

I gathered some more cows an' headed them in the same direction as the others. One of these cows was limpin' pretty bad an' needin' a little doctorin' for foot rot.

I decided that rather than ropin' her on the spot an' doctorin' her right there, I'd get her as close to the other cows as I could, then help her.

We got to where the other cattle was an' I started the whole herd again. It had taken me almost a full day to do what I had originally thought I could do in half a day. I was plumb disgusted with myself.

We had about a mile to go when I decided to catch the cow with foot rot. I figured if I had to tough a time of it, I could leave her an' get her another day. For some reason or another, everything I done today was harder than usual an' most of the time I'd end up in some sort of jackpot. I figured things might go a little easier if I didn't try so hard.

I got my rope down an' headed for the cow with foot rot. Now, when I first seen her, she seemed pretty lame, but when I was tryin' to catch her, she acted like she didn't have anything wrong with her. It took me a couple of tries, but I finally got a rope on her. Again, it looked like a situation where the cure was worse than the disease an' when I did get her caught, she was so tired, I didn't even have to get off the horse to give her a shot. She just laid there.

I got done, got my rope off an' headed back towards camp. This had been a long, hard day an' there wasn't no reason to make it worse. The cow that I'd freed from the cattle guard earlier an' was in the wrong place could wait 'till tomorrow. It had been a tough day.

First Bronc Ride

I was a little nervous about my first bronc ride. I had rode a bronc on the ranch, sometimes with success, sometimes without much success. But I was young, and my aspiration was to be a bronc rider. I wasn't scared of what might happen in the arena, I was scared of what the spectators might think, more a case of stage fright than anything else.

The small town up the road a few miles held a rodeo each year. Some wild horses were run in a few days before the rodeo, and cows and calves were furnished by local farmers for the roping and bull or cow riding, as the case might be. At this little rodeo, the cows sometimes had to be used as bulls for the bull riding.

Dick and I were both 12 or 13 at the time and we were taking fairly elaborate preparations for the upcoming rodeo. Whenever we could, we would run some 700 or 800 pound Holstein steers into a smaller corral so as we could practice our "bull" riding. We didn't have a chute, but by maneuvering a steer very carefully, we could catch him between the fence and the gate. As far as a chute goes, it worked, but it was more triangular in shape and it left a lot to be desired.

It was a lot of fun riding them steers, but it wasn't much fun when we got caught. I don't really know what hurt the most, getting bucked off them steers or getting caught by the foreman and accepting the punishment he doled out.

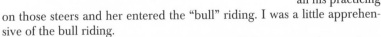

Finally the big day of the little rodeo arrived. Dick wasn't much interested in getting entered in the bronc riding, he'd really done all his practicing on those steers and her entered the "bull" riding. I was a little apprehensive of the bull riding.

The day before, while practicing, a big Holstien steer slammed me down pretty hard in the corral. I was having some second thoughts about entering the "bull" riding, but I hadn't been bucked off a horse for sometime so I entered the bareback bronc riding.

The mustangs used for the bronc riding were pretty wild. Some had been run in before and bucked out in previous years, but by and large they were untried broncs.

I drawed a little sorrel mare. She sure didn't resemble the picturesque mustang that most people imagine. Her hair was still shaggy and it was the middle of summer. She was crooked in her hind legs and looked pretty rough all over.

In the chute, she wasn't to sensible and we had to tie up her head. I remember thinking that I was glad we didn't have to use the improvised chute like we had when we practiced on the steers. When I called for the gate, one of the hands let go on her head. We had a pretty wild time in the chute, but cleared without any further trouble.

Once away from the chute, the little mare lined out pretty good, made a couple of jumps, then started running. And she could run fast.

We made the whistle without any problem, the problem soon became apparent, how to get off! The pickup man couldn't catch us, and he had the inside circle. We made about four runs around the arena and when the pickup man saw he couldn't reach us, he hollered, "Take the fence if you can get it!"

Now I had considered the various means of getting off, and didn't really like two of the three alternatives. But we were taking a lot of time. The first alternative was just bailing off, but as fast as we were going, I was a little nervous about it. The second was taking the fence as the pickup man suggested, but that didn't really appeal to me. The third option, the ideal one, was to have the pickup man pluck me off this bronc and set me gently on the ground, on my feet.

The last option was the most desirable, but the least likely. When it was suggested I take the fence, I started looking for a good place. The fence was going by pretty fast and every time I picked a likely spot, it went past before I could act. Finally, in desperation, I just stuck out my free hand and took the first available post.

For a split second, I was off. Then I realizes what I had forgot to do– namely, let go of my rigging!

I was stretched out between an arena fence post and the fast departing mare. It didn't last long however, because at the same instant my hand came loose from the rigging, I lost my grip on the post. For a fraction of a second, I was suspended in mid air, but not for long, I had rough meeting with the ground.

When I got to the end of the arena, the mare was still running around. I'd ripped my shirt and my glove and I came to the conclusion that taking the fence was just as bad as being bucked off, maybe worse.

I also came to the conclusion that the next time I had the opportunity to pick when and where I dismounted a bronc in a rodeo, I was going to pick a place closer to chutes. I'd had a long walk and didn't really go any-where.

Anniversary

Some years ago, we celebrated our first anniversary with a day of gifts, surprises, relaxing and an evening of dining and dancing.

Getting ready for bed that night, my wife asked me how much money I had spent on the day.

"One hundred dollars," I replied.

"You spent one hundred dollars on our first anniversary?"

"Yes," I answered.

"Well, at the rate of one hundred dollars a year, I can't wait until we've been married 9 or 10 years!"

Jerk - Line

"I guess if he starts buckin', I can take this here jerk-line, take a couple of wraps around this here horn, an' that will hold his head up." My neighbor, Dave, sounded fairly confident with his plan.

"If you can do it fast enough, it might work," I said, as positively as possible. Sounded like he would have to be a whole lot faster than I am to make it work.

We were gathering cows an' goin' to push them up the mountain a little farther. I was ridin' Dave's good horse, Rangoon, an' Dave was ridin' a pretty fair lookin' buckskin colt that he'd just started just today.

"Now that you've got him started, if you can keep him goin', you'll make a pretty good horse out of that knothead," I said. This was the first actual ride that had been made on the colt.

The colt had been tried a time or two by some long-haired kids that smoked funny cigarettes. I don't think they were trying to break him, just seein' who could stay on longest, 'cause he did learn how to buck an' how to do a good job of it.

The "jerk-line" Dave referred to was a lead rope about 20 feet long. Dave was starting this colt in a snaffle bit an' had a halter underneath the headstall. Not exactly the way I would have done it, but I wasn't ridin' the horse.

I had some colts of my own that needed ridin', but we brought Rangoon so as we'd have a good snubbin' horse. Dave figured once he was on, he could handle about anything.

We started out at a slow easy lope an' just played out enough of the "jerk-line" so as I could help control the colt if needed an' the horses wouldn't be trippin' over each other. We kept the lope up until the colt started to tire some, then slowed it down to a fast trot. I figured if we got the colt tired to start with, Dave might not have too many problems with the horse the rest of the day.

We got the colt tired, but before I turned them loose, I thought I'd have a little fun with Dave.

"You know," I says, "I used to be in the dude business an' sometimes I'd have to lead some little kid around on horse, sorta like we're doin' now. Some of them kids just couldn't keep their horse from puttin' his head down an' gettin' a bite to eat. Or they couldn't keep the horse from wonderin' out through the willows to scratch his belly."

"I believe I can handle him from here on out," said Dave.

"Then sometimes," I continued, "they'd be some feller goofin' off towards the end of the line an' if he was endangerin' the ride for the other dudes, I'd lead him on in, sorta like we're doin' now."

"I know I can handle him from here on out," said Dave, givin' me a dirty look.

We'd stopped the horses to let them blow an' I was about ten feet from Dave an' the buckskin.

"You want to be weaned?"

"I would like to ride over that hill an' enjoy a nice quiet morning ride," said Dave with extra emphasis on the word quiet and an even dirtier look at me than before.

"Well, I'll turn you loose," I says as I flipped the end of the lead rope to him. "But only if you promise to be a good boy for the rest of the day!"

The buckskin shied some an' Dave didn't have time to give me a dirty look what with catchin' the end of the lead rope am' keepin' his horse under control. But the buckskin didn't buck, an' I figured they'd be alright the rest of the day unless they hit some major jackpot.

We made a cow gather that day. I tried to at least stay within eyesight of Dave, just in case he needed some help with his colt. As it was, Dave an' the buckskin was makin' a lot of extra work for themselves an' me, 'cause the colt didn't know anything about turnin', stoppin', or even slowin' down. I managed to give him a good hand there, correctin' his mistakes an' even cussin' him for causin' so much extra work. 'Course I knew where the extra work was comin' from, but just couldn't resist the temptation to have a little fun at his expense. I knew he was goin' to be just as tired as that colt when we got through.

We gathered enough cows and started up the mountain when it happened. I don't know what set the buckskin off, I missed it. The sound of stirrup leathers poppin' over an empty saddle is what drew my attention to the fact that something was wrong. By the time I looked to catch the action, it was over.

Dave was layin' on the ground an' from the position he was in, I figured he'd busted a hip or something. The buckskin had hit a runnin' buck an' headed in the general direction of camp.

"Smart horse," I thought as I started out after the colt. "He just wanted to quit early today, already figured out how to do it an' headed for camp."

Dave looked to be in considerable pain as Rangoon an' me run by him after the buckskin. The colt had a big enough head start that it gave me some time to think. These were Dave's cows, Dave's horses, Dave's outfit, an' if he was hurt bad enough, I'd have to leave everything, get him back to camp an' start all over tomorrow. If he could stand the pain a little longer, I could push the cows a little farther up the mountain, put them through a cross fence an' not have to do everything all over again.

I got the buckskin caught an' started back to where I left Dave. I was surprised an' relieved to see Dave limpin' around. At least the day wasn't wasted.

"What happened?"

"Me an' the horse parted company," said Dave.

"I gathered that! What set him off?"

"I been ridin' on this mountain all my life. An' all my life I been told never to ride a colt down the steep side of one of these stock ponds. I forgot. I guess the saddle slid forward an' pinched him a little."

"Good thing that saddle didn't bite him," I said. "From the looks of things, if it had of bit him, he'd of killed you." Dave didn't look very good.

"What happened to your jerk-line idea?"

"Didn't work," answered Dave.

Dave didn't pay extra for ridin' colts, but I volunteered to swap horses with him for the rest of the day. "You know," I concluded, "I got these spurs on, an' I know how to use 'em. We could sure teach that colt a good lesson an' make it stick."

"No," says Dave. "I about got him where I want him an' don't want him ruined."

I had to think about that one.

We snubbed the buckskin an' Dave got back on. We got our cows moved without further mishap or excitement. On the way back to camp, I got to thinkin' about swappin' horses with Dave. I'm real relieved that Dave an' me didn't swap horses. I would have hated for him to go around tellin' everybody that he had to take the buck out of that buckskin so as I could ride him.

Dancin' Fool

The rodeo dance was the big thing for the evening. The rodeo was over an' the bull I'd drawed hadn't treated me to well. I was still tryin' to figure out how I could have hurt so many muscles in such a short time.

I'd got a shower at the motel, rubbed a little liniment on the hurtin' muscles, an' now, with a clean shirt, a shave an' to much strong after shave, I was hobblin' into the dance hall. I figured if I kept movin', I wouldn't get to stiff.

I was doin' pretty good at the dance, two out of three an' that's better than what I did at the rodeo, an' I even danced a couple to the jukebox when the band took a break.

I was havin' a real good time an' once I got a gal out on the dance floor, I sure didn't want to let her go, so I kept askin' her to dance an' she kept acceptin'.

At one point, right after I asked her to dance another one, she made the remark, "You're just a dancin' fool, aren't you?"

I thought about it a minute, then said, "Well I guess you're half right."

She agreed, an I felt fairly comfortable about it until I got to thinkin' about it later. An' the more I thought about it, the worse it got. I don't know whether she was agreein' with me that I liked to dance or agreein' that I was a fool! And, I still don't know!

Keep Talkin'

I didn't know who would go with a 40-year-old man who'd been married twice, was payin' child support on 5 kids, drove a pickup with more than two hundred thousand miles on it, was in debt up to his ears, rode bulls (sometimes not very long), an' didn't drink, but if she was around, I was goin' to find her. I was lookin' for a date to go to the rodeo dance afterwards.

I asked an ol' gal, who sorta had me interested, if she'd like to go to the rodeo with me. She seemed sorta interested, but wouldn't commit herself with a simple yes or no. She hadn't come up with a blunt "no" so I figured I still had a chance.

Appealing to some sense she might have about being associated with a winner or at least some sort of personality, I says, as casually as possible, "I guess you know I'm entered in the bull ridin'."

That comment didn't seem to impress her much, but she still hadn't said no. I could see that I still had to do some talkin' to convince her to go.

I thought I might appeal to her sense of humanity, so I said, "You know if I got hurt ridin' that bull, I'd need somebody to drive me home." Well, that comment didn't impress her much either an' I could see that I was goin' to have to do more talkin'. She was makin' me go the distance an' I got to figurin' that I'd better make some sort of appeal to all of her, as I was runnin' out of things to say.

So I says to her, "You know, if you was kind enough to go to the rodeo with me, an' if I did get hurt ridin' bulls, an' you was kind enough to get me home, you probably wouldn't mind doin' the irrigating either!"

Now, I don't know if she didn't like rodeo or irrigatin', but I ended up goin' to the rodeo alone, missin' the dance an' changin' the water by myself!

Gone Fishin'

"It would really be nice if we could catch up our horses an' just take off, spend a weekend fishin' up in them Baldie Mountains." It was my new brother-in-law, Danny. "I could use some time relaxin'," he continues, "All the work seems to be pilin' up on me this spring."

Danny had come over to borrow some dehorners and equipment to get his branding done.

"I'm not really a fisherman," I said. "But I'd go an' tend camp for you. That would be my idea of relaxin'."

"Get your horse an' we'll do it. I'll get my brandin' out of the way an' we can go this coming weekend."

"Just catchin' my horse might be more of a job than I want. It took me more than half a day just to run him out of that hayfield into that pasture the other day. I couldn't even get close enough to throw a rope at him. He's wintered out all year, forgot what oats is and really seemed to enjoy runnin' my tail off. Besides that, I was cuttin' the inside circle on him."

Danny asked, "Can you catch him with another horse?"

"Sure," I replied. "He's not really that fast. He just relishes in runnin' faster an' longer than I am even interested in attempting."

"I can bring a horse over an' we'll get him caught," said Danny. "We'll go fishin' this weekend."

Danny showed up the next day with a horse an' it didn't take long to catch my horse. He came right into the corral with Danny's horse an' once the gate was shut, he was captured.

I'd had this horse for about ten years. He was started when I got him and I just got on and went to work. He worked real good in a hackamore an I'd never put a bit in his mouth. He still acted a little "broncy" when he was caught, snortin' an' blowin', but all in all he was a pretty fair horse, a good traveler an' sensible. He was hard to catch, but he was captured now.

We decided it would be easier for Danny to haul my horse over to his place. We could leave from there to go fishin' Saturday morning. Danny got a few extra things he needed for brandin' an' his last words were, "I'll have the brandin' done this week. We'll have some coffee at the ranch Saturday morning an' leave about seven. All that you'll need is your saddle an' bedroll, I've got everything else."

The rest of the week slowly drug by. I stayed busy but my mind kept daydreaming about a weekend with nothing to do, just ride up on some lake in the Baldies, set up a camp, do little cookin' an' relax a lot. I was lookin' forward to a real enjoyable weekend.

Saturday morning came and I found myself excited about goin' fishin'. I was up and off to Danny's early, before I even had my coffee, knowing I could get coffee at Danny's.

But Danny wasn't even up when I arrived. I got him up an' lined him out makin' coffee then went down to the corrals. I caught my horse and got him saddled. I'd never been fishin' before and didn't know exactly what to do or what we needed.

I went back to the house to get some coffee and see what I could do to help get ready. The coffee was perking and Danny was mumbling something about things never going just right!

"What's up?" I asked. I'd just recently married into this family, didn't really know anybody and they didn't really know anything about me, except that I was a cowboy. I didn't know it at the time, but I was going to get an education about my wife's family, starting that day.

"Things didn't work out just right last week," said Danny. "I got busy an' didn't get the brandin' done. Things just seem to pile up on me."

"So, what's the plan?"

"You can go fishin'. I'll tell you how to get to a good spot. I've got some extra help coming to help brand, I've got to get that out of the way."

"I really ain't to interested in goin' fishin' alone," I said. "Suppose I helped you brand, then we could go?"

"I can always use help with the cattle," said Danny, smiling. "But I'd feel funny havin' you help me brand when you want to go fishin'."

What Danny didn't realize was that I didn't want to go fishin', I wanted to go relaxin'. I told Danny, "If I help you with your brandin', we'll get done faster then we can go relax... er, fishin'. I've got all I need, my horse, saddle, bedroll an' you've got my dehorners an' that stuff. We can make fast work out of them calves, although I really should have my own irons."

"Your own irons? What do you need with them? These are my calves we're brandin'."

"Well," I says, "We could slap my brand on a few of them calves if your irons got cold. Then we could go fishin' faster."

"We'll see about the fishin'," said Danny, "But each one of those calves should be packin' the same brand that it's mama has."

Some of Danny's extra help started showing up and more coffee was made. This was beginning to look like a coffee shop rather than a cattle outfit. I didn't know how many cattle Danny had, but was beginning to suspect he figured it would go a lot faster if he had three men and a boy for each calf that needed to be branded.

The coffee was drank up and reluctantly everyone agreed that it was about time to get started. I hadn't used my horse all winter and most everybody was interested in seeing if he'd buck at least once a year, most often during the first, second or third time I rode him.

He did have a hump in his back when I got on him, but I eased him around the corral some, did a few stops an' turns and was real pleased that he didn't seem to want to buck. He might have bucked if I'd encouraged him.

For some reason or other, Danny took a liking to my horse. He wanted to own him and he offered me five hundred dollars for him. I just laughed when I told him I'd turned down nine hundred just last fall. When Danny heard this, he upped his bid to a thousand. I told him the horse wasn't for sale at any price and Danny offered eleven hundred dollars, just like he hadn't heard.

I was trying to say no nicely, but Danny was persistent. At thirteen hundred dollars, Danny's wife left disgustedly to saddle her own horse. At fifteen hundred, I decided to put an end to the impromptu bidding.

"Do you want to pay in cash or by check?"

Danny stammered for a while and finally said, "I guess I'd have to give you a check right now."

"Well, a check won't do me any good on a fishin' trip. Besides, the horse ain't for sale today at any price. Now lets get them calves branded so we can go relax.., er, fishin'.'"

With all the help, we didn't have much trouble corralling the cows. It might have been easier to capture the cattle without so much help. We sorted off the calves, built a fire and delegated duties to everyone. With all this help, I figured it wouldn't take long to brand these calves.

Danny wanted me to do the roping and I began to have some doubts as to how long this job was going to take. I'm not known for outstanding ability in roping.

The only thing these guys knew about me was that I was a cowboy, and I sure wanted them to know that I was a good one. So I decided that I was going to drag only those calves up to the fire that I had caught by both hind legs.

The roping was fairly easy in the corral. There weren't any rocks, tall grass, trees or cows in the way. The calves mingled at the far end of the corral away from the fire and it was easy roping.

When I got to where I had about half the calves done, I offered to let someone else rope, but nobody seemed interested and they said things were going well and I should keep roping. Surprisingly, I hadn't missed many throws, although I'd had to lay a trap and wait for a calf to step into it. Fishin', I'd thought to myself. But the calves weren't to wild because they'd had a rope slapped up along side their flanks.

With about three quarters of the roping done, I decided to let someone else do the roping. I was getting a little tired anyways. One of Danny's helpers, John, decided he could do it. That's when I got surprised.

I'd taken a lot of care to make sure every calf I'd roped was done according to the book, real professional; lay a trap, make sure the calf had both hind legs in it, pick up the slack, dally and turn the horse. I was trying to make everything real smooth.

But John, well John was a disappointment. I thought these guys were pretty good cowboys but John wasn't showing me anything with his roping. He was bringing in calves anyway he could catch them, by one leg, both legs, the head, even one caught around the middle. And as far as the dallying, half a turn around the saddle horn seemed to do it most of the time and he even drug a few of the smaller calves with his rope over his shoulder. I was really disappointed, especially when nobody seemed to notice how much care I had taken to bring in the calves I roped by both hind feet.

We finally got the calves done. We ran the cows through, ear-tagged each one with a fly control tag, cut off a few horns and gave a few shots. When we got done it was after noon and I figured it was time to go fishin'. But it wasn't. The women fixed dinner.

My day of relaxing was turning into a day of work. And after a big dinner, I didn't feel like doing anything. I cornered Danny and asked him about going fishin'.

"It's really to late to go fishin' today,' answered Danny. "But if you really want to go fishin', I'll lend you a pole an' you can go down to the stock watering pond an' fish. I stocked it a couple of years ago and there are some big ones down there."

"But Danny, you don't understand. I don't care if I go fishin' or not, I want to go relaxin'. That was my original idea, just relaxin'!"

"That's OK too. You can do a lot of relaxin' down at the pond an' you might even catch something."

Slowly, I rode my horse down to the pond. I had a fishin' pole but didn't know how to use it. I got to the pond, hobbled my horse and took a good long nap.

That night as I drove home, I got it figured out. I had been set up. Yes, I did get some relaxing, a nap but I put in a pretty good days work for lunch. I came to the conclusion that I was going to have to watch this family. Fishin' trips would definitely be out of the question in the future. The only fishin' I really did was for some of them calves heels, and it was fairly successful. But I did come to the conclusion that I was going to have to watch this family. I sure didn't want to be suckered into doing all of Danny's work in the future. And there were three other brother-in-laws to contend with that I hadn't even met!

ARTIST: R. LOREN SCHMIDT

R. Loren Schmidt is a "Cowboy Artist" in the true sense of the word. Loren not only has been drawing and painting since childhood, he has been a full-time cowboy most of his life. Loren was born in 1953 in Bridgeport, Nebraska where his family owned and operated a large cattle ranch. Loren was immersed in the cowboy way of life at an early age, but his artistic promise was also evident as a youngster. Loren graduated from Montana State University in 1979 with a degree in Art Education. Following graduation, he worked for the Hammer Bar4/320 Ranch near Yellowstone National Park as a cow camp cowboy. This was a remote and lonely job, with the nearest road some 20 miles away. However, this gave Loren an opportunity to hone his artistic skill and to absorb what living with nature has to offer the artistic mind.

In 1990, Loren with the encouragement of Tom Coblentz of Elk Horn Art Gallery in Winter Park, Colorado and other artist friends, decided to make the commitment to a full-time career in fine art. Since making this decision, his progress has been rapid and he knows and loves—the contemporary western cowboy, horses, cattle, wildlife and scenery—all integral parts of his life. These real life experiences are expressed in Loren's pen and ink drawings contained in this book.